Prentice Hall Realidades B

Communication Workbook with Test Preparation

D1319434

PEARSON

Boston, Massachusetts   Chandler, Arizona   Glenview, Illinois   Upper Saddle River, New Jersey

Art and Map Credits

Page 135: © Dave Albers/Illustration Works, Inc.; **Page 141:** Ted Smykal; **Page 153:** (map) Ted Smykal; **Page 171:** (map) Ted Smykal

Copyright © Pearson Education, Inc., or its affiliates. All Rights Reserved. Printed in the United States of America. This publication is protected by copyright, and permission should be obtained from the publisher prior to any prohibited reproduction, storage in a retrieval system, or transmission in any form or by any means, electronic, mechanical, photocopying, recording, or likewise. For information regarding permissions, write to Rights Management & Contracts, Pearson Education, Inc., One Lake Street, Upper Saddle River, New Jersey 07458.

Pearson, Prentice Hall, and Pearson Prentice Hall are trademarks, in the U.S. and/or other countries, of Pearson Education, Inc., or its affiliates.

ISBN-13: 978-0-13-322575-4

ISBN-10:   0-13-322575-5

1 2 3 4 5 6 7 8 9 10 V0N4 16 15 14 13 12

Table of Contents

Writing, Audio, and Video Activities   v

Test Preparation   119

© Pearson Education, Inc. All rights reserved.

Prentice Hall Realidades B

Writing, Audio & Video Activities

PEARSON

Boston, Massachusetts   Chandler, Arizona   Glenview, Illinois   Upper Saddle River, New Jersey

Table of Contents

Tema 5: Fiesta en familia

Capítulo 5A: Una fiesta de cumpleaños

Video Activities 1

Audio Activities 4

Writing Activities 8

Capítulo 5B: ¡Vamos a un restaurante!

Video Activities 12

Audio Activities 15

Writing Activities 18

Tema 6: La casa

Capítulo 6A: En mi dormitorio

Video Activities 22

Audio Activities 25

Writing Activities 29

Capítulo 6B: ¿Cómo es tu casa?

Video Activities 33

Audio Activities 36

Writing Activities 39

© Pearson Education, Inc. All rights reserved.

Tema 7: De compras

Capítulo 7A: ¿Cuánto cuesta?

Video Activities 43

Audio Activities 46

Writing Activities 49

Capítulo 7B: ¡Qué regalo!

Video Activities 53

Audio Activities 56

Writing Activities 59

Tema 8: Experiencias

Capítulo 8A: De vacaciones

Video Activities 63

Audio Activities 66

Writing Activities 69

Capítulo 8B: Ayudando en la comunidad

Video Activities 73

Audio Activities 76

Writing Activities 79

© Pearson Education, Inc. All rights reserved.

Tema 9: Medios de comunicación

Capítulo 9A: El cine y la televisión

Video Activities 83

Audio Activities 86

Writing Activities 89

Capítulo 9B: La tecnología

Video Activities 93

Audio Activities 96

Writing Activities 98

© Pearson Education, Inc. All rights reserved.

Antes de ver el video

Actividad 1

Look at this family tree. Label each person with his or her relationship to Ricardo.

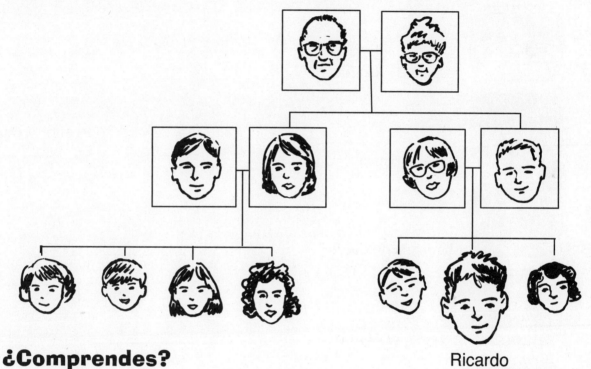

Ricardo

¿Comprendes?

Actividad 2

Cristina had a birthday party with some of her family members. How much do you remember about that party? Write **cierto** or **falso** next to each statement.

1. Angélica hace un video de la fiesta de su hermano. _____

2. El papá de Cristina saca fotos de la fiesta. _____

3. A Gabriel le gustan los deportes. _____

4. El perro de Cristina se llama Piñata. _____

5. La abuela de Cristina decora la fiesta con papel picado. _____

6. Capitán es muy sociable, le encanta estar con la familia. _____

7. Carolina es la hermana de Gabriel y Angélica. _____

8. Ricardo es el abuelo de Esteban. _____

© Pearson Education, Inc. All rights reserved.

Realidades Ⓑ

Capítulo 5A

Nombre _____

Hora _____

Fecha _____

VIDEO

Actividad 3

Who is being described? Write his or her name next to the description.

Description	Name

1. esposa de Ricardo _____

2. tío de Cristina _____

3. hermana de Gabriel _____

4. esposa de Andrés _____

5. primo de Angélica _____

6. hermana mayor de Esteban _____

7. abuelo de Cristina _____

© Pearson Education, Inc. All rights reserved.

Y, ¿qué más?

Actividad 4

At Cristina's party we met many family members. Why don't you introduce your family, too?
Write three sentences about your family or a family you know well. Follow the examples below.

Yo vivo en mi casa con mi mamá y mi hermano.

TÚ: _____

Mi hermano se llama Martín y tiene 10 años.

TÚ: _____

Yo tengo muchos primos y primas.

TÚ: _____

The lyrics for "Las mañanitas" as sung on the video are:

Éstas son las mañanitas que cantaba el rey David
a las muchachas bonitas, te las cantamos a ti.
Despierta, mi bien, despierta, mira que ya amaneció,
ya los pajarillos cantan, la luna ya se metió.

These are the early morning birthday songs
that King David used to sing
to pretty girls, and so we sing them to you.
Wake up, my dear, wake up, look, dawn has already come,
the little birds are singing, the moon is gone.

© Pearson Education, Inc. All rights reserved.

Realidades B

Capítulo 5A

Nombre _____

Fecha _____

Hora _____

AUDIO

Actividad 5

Beto is showing Raúl a picture of his family at a birthday party. Identify as many people as you can and write their names and relationship to Beto under the pictures. If Beto refers to a pet, simply write the pet's name under the picture. You will hear this conversation twice.

© Pearson Education, Inc. All rights reserved.

Actividad 6

You are chosen to participate in a popular radio quiz show on a local Spanish radio station. When it is your turn, you are happy to hear that your questions are in the category of **FAMILIA**. See if you can answer all of the questions correctly on the entry card below. Each question becomes a little more difficult. You will hear each set of questions twice.

1. _____

2. _____

3. _____

4. _____

5. _____

Actividad 7

Listen as three brothers talk to their mother after school. Try to fill in all of the squares in the grid with the correct information about Julio, Mateo, and Víctor. Remember, you might not hear the information given in the same order as it appears in the grid. You will hear this conversation twice.

	¿Cuántos años tiene?	¿Qué le gusta hacer?	¿Qué tiene que hacer?	¿Qué tiene en la mochila?
Julio				
Mateo				
Víctor				

© Pearson Education, Inc. All rights reserved.

Nombre _____

Hora _____

Fecha _____

AUDIO

Actividad 8

Listen as two students tell their host families in Chile about their own families back home. As you listen to both of them, see if you can tell which family is being described. Put a check mark in the appropriate box on the grid. You will hear each set of statements twice.

La familia Gómez

La familia Sora

	1	2	3	4	5	6	7	8
La familia Gómez								
La familia Sora								

© Pearson Education, Inc. All rights reserved.

AUDIO

Actividad 9

Listen to the following phone calls to Ana, a favorite local talk show host. Each caller has a problem with someone in his or her family. As you listen to each caller, take notes on his or her problems. After all of the callers have spoken, write a sentence of advice for each caller. You may write your advice in English. You will hear each set of statements twice.

	PROBLEMA	CONSEJO
Maritza		
Armando		
Andrés		
María Luisa		

© Pearson Education, Inc. All rights reserved.

WRITING

Actividad 10

Look at the pages from the Rulfo family photo album below. Then, write one or two sentences describing the people in each photo. What is their relationship to each other? What do you think they are like, based on the pictures?

1. Foto 1

_____

_____

_____

2. Foto 2

_____

_____

_____

3. Foto 3

_____

_____

_____

© Pearson Education, Inc. All rights reserved.

Realidades **B**

Capítulo 5A

Nombre _____

Fecha _____

Hora _____

WRITING

Actividad 11

People have many obligations during the day. Using **tener que**, write what you think the following people have to do at the time of day or place given. Follow the model.

> **Modelo** mi padre / a las 7:00 de la mañana
>
> *Mi padre tiene que desayunar a las siete de la mañana.*

1. yo / a las 7:30 de la mañana

_____

2. tú / en la clase de español

_____

3. los estudiantes / en la clase de inglés

_____

4. el profesor / en la clase de matemáticas

_____

5. las personas de la escuela / a las doce de la tarde (al mediodía)

_____

6. Uds. / en la clase de arte

_____

7. los estudiantes malos / en la clase de educación física

_____

8. mi amigo / a las 3:00 de la tarde

_____

9. mis hermanos y yo / a las 5:00 de la tarde

_____

10. mi familia / a las 6:00 de la tarde

_____

© Pearson Education, Inc. All rights reserved.

Realidades Ⓑ

Capítulo 5A

Nombre _____

Fecha _____

Hora _____

WRITING

Actividad 12

A. Your family tree is very complex. It takes many links to connect everyone in the family. Using possessive adjectives, write 10 sentences about how people are related in your family. Use the model to help you.

Modelo	*Mi tío tiene dos hijos.*
	Mi abuelo es el padre de mi tía.

1. _____

2. _____

3. _____

4. _____

5. _____

6. _____

7. _____

8. _____

9. _____

10. _____

B. Now, draw your family tree.

© Pearson Education, Inc. All rights reserved.

Realidades B

Capítulo 5A

Nombre _____

Hora _____

Fecha _____

WRITING

Actividad 13

Your pen pal from Argentina has asked you to tell her about a member of your family. First, tell her the person's name, age, and relationship to you. Then, describe what the person is like.

Once you finish writing, read your description and check to make sure that all the words are spelled correctly and that you have used accents where necessary. Also, check to make sure the endings of the adjectives agree with the nouns they are describing.

> *Hola, Ana Sofía:*
>
> _____
>
> _____
>
> _____
>
> _____
>
> _____
>
> _____
>
> _____
>
> _____
>
> _____
>
> _____
>
> *Saludos,*
>
> _____

© Pearson Education, Inc. All rights reserved.

Realidades B

Capítulo 5B

Nombre _____

Hora _____

Fecha _____

VIDEO

Antes de ver el video

Actividad 1

Select from the word bank the appropriate nouns to write under each heading: things needed to set the table, things to eat, and things to drink.

menú	tacos	tenedor	flan
enchiladas	limonada	servilleta	postre
café	refresco	cuchillo	jugo de naranja

Para poner la mesa   **Para comer**   **Para beber**

_____   _____   _____

_____   _____   _____

_____   _____   _____

_____   _____   _____

¿Comprendes?

Actividad 2

Angélica's family is having dinner at the restaurant **México Lindo**. Find the best choice to complete each statement by writing the letter in the space provided.

1. El camarero está nervioso; _____

   a. tiene mucho trabajo.

   b. es su primer día de trabajo.

   c. tiene sueño.

2. El papá de Angélica pide un té helado _____

   a. porque tiene calor.

   b. porque es delicioso.

   c. porque tiene frío.

© Pearson Education, Inc. All rights reserved.

Realidades B

Capítulo 5B

Nombre _____

Hora _____

Fecha _____

VIDEO

3. La mamá de Angélica pide de postre _____

   a. arroz con pollo.

   b. tacos de bistec.

   c. flan.

4. La mamá de Angélica necesita _____

   a. una servilleta.

   b. el menú.

   c. un cuchillo y un tenedor.

Actividad 3

Match each person with the things he or she ordered. Write the letter of the foods and beverages in the spaces provided.

1. Mamá _____   a. jugo de naranja y fajitas de pollo

2. Angélica _____   b. enchiladas

3. Papá _____   c. café, ensalada de frutas y flan

4. Esteban _____   d. té helado, tacos de bistec y café

5. Cristina _____   e. refresco y arroz con pollo

6. Sr. del pelo castaño _____   f. hamburguesa y refresco

© Pearson Education, Inc. All rights reserved.

Y, ¿qué más?

Actividad 4

You and your friend Graciela are having dinner at a Mexican restaurant with your family. Graciela doesn't speak Spanish, so your mom orders dinner for her. Then, you give your order. Look at the menu to see your options, then write your order in the space provided in the dialogue below.

MENÚ		
BEBIDAS	**PLATO PRINCIPAL**	**POSTRES**
Refrescos	Enchiladas	Flan
Jugo de naranja	Tacos de carne/pollo	Helado
Té helado/caliente	Fajitas de carne/pollo	Frutas frescas
Café	Burritos	

CAMARERO: ¿Qué van a pedir para beber?

MAMÁ: La joven quiere un jugo de naranja, y yo quiero un refresco.

TÚ: _____

CAMARERO: ¿Qué quieren pedir para el plato principal?

MAMÁ: Para la joven enchiladas, y yo quiero arroz con pollo.

TÚ: _____

CAMARERO: ¿Quieren pedir algo de postre?

MAMÁ: Para la joven un flan. Yo no quiero nada, gracias.

TÚ: _____

© Pearson Education, Inc. All rights reserved.

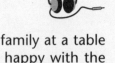

Actividad 5

You are delighted to find out that you can understand a conversation that a family at a table near you in a restaurant is having in Spanish. The family doesn't seem very happy with the waiter. Listen to find out what each family member is upset about. By looking at the pictures in the grid below, check off the item that is causing the problem. You will hear each conversation twice.

Actividad 6

Five young people go to a department store to buy hats (**sombreros**) as presents for their friends. Listen as each person describes the person he or she is buying the present for. Write the name of each person described under the hat that best matches that person. You will hear each conversation twice.

© Pearson Education, Inc. All rights reserved.

Realidades **B**

Capítulo 5B

Nombre _____

Hora _____

Fecha _____

AUDIO

 sociable,
deportista,
atrevido(a)

_____

 romántico(a),
talentoso(a),
paciente

_____

serio(a),
trabajador(a),
práctico(a)

_____

 elegante,
divertido(a),
simpático(a)

_____

 aventurero(a),
atrevido(a),
interesante

_____

Actividad 7

Listen as a group of friends discuss Julia's upcoming surprise birthday party. Look at the list of party items. Write the name of each person next to the item that he or she is bringing. Circle any item that still needs to be assigned. You will hear this conversation twice.

Los platos _____ Los refrescos _____ Las servilletas _____

Los vasos _____ Los globos _____ El postre _____

Los tenedores _____ La piñata _____ Las flores _____

Las cucharas _____ Las luces _____ El helado _____

Actividad 8

Iván knows many different people from various places. Listen to him describe these people. Fill in the chart as you hear each piece of information given. You will hear each set of statements twice.

	¿De dónde es/son?	¿Dónde está(n)?	¿Está(n) contento/a/os/as?
Juanita			
Los tíos			
Iván y su familia			
Felipe			
Juanita y Julie			

© Pearson Education, Inc. All rights reserved.

Realidades **B**

Capítulo 5B

Nombre _____

Fecha _____

Hora _____

AUDIO

Actividad 9

Listen as a girl describes a photo of a party to her friend who was unable to attend. Write the names of each person described on the line that corresponds to each picture. You will hear the dialogues twice.

A. _____   D. _____

B. _____   E. _____

C. _____   F. _____

© Pearson Education, Inc. All rights reserved.

WRITING

Actividad 10

Draw a picture of yourself and three other people in your family. Then, write a description of the person below each picture. You can draw imaginary family members if you prefer.

1.

_____ Yo _____

_____

_____

_____

_____

_____

_____

2.

_____

_____

_____

_____

_____

_____

_____

3.

_____

_____

_____

_____

_____

_____

_____

4.

_____

_____

_____

_____

_____

_____

_____

© Pearson Education, Inc. All rights reserved.

Realidades B

Capítulo 5B

Nombre _____

Hora _____

Fecha _____

WRITING

Actividad 11

In preparation for their upcoming party, Juan and Elisa are talking on the phone about who is coming and what each guest is bringing. Read Elisa's guest list below, then complete the friends' conversation by writing sentences that include the correct form of either **venir** or **traer**.

Nuestra fiesta

Anita - la pizza
Pablo y José - la salsa
Jorge y Marta - la limonada y los refrescos
Luisa y Marcos - las galletas de chocolate
Nosotros - la carne

JUAN: ¿Anita viene a la fiesta el sábado?

ELISA: _____.

JUAN: ¡Qué bien! ¿También van a venir Pablo y José?

ELISA: Sí. Ellos _____.

JUAN: ¿Qué traen ellos?

ELISA: _____.

JUAN: Bien. Y ¿quién trae las bebidas?

ELISA: Pues, _____.

JUAN: Sí. Ahora, ¿quiénes traen el postre?

ELISA: _____.

JUAN: ¡Perfecto! ¿Y nosotros? ¿_____?

ELISA: ¡Traemos la carne, por supuesto!

© Pearson Education, Inc. All rights reserved.

Nombre _____ Hora _____

Fecha _____

WRITING

Actividad 12

Describe the following people. Consider their mood and location, their personality and appearance. Be creative and use the pictures and model to help you.

Modelo

Él es joven. Su pelo es corto y negro.

Es un chico estudioso.

Está en casa ahora porque está enfermo.

1. _____
   _____
   _____
   _____

2. _____
   _____
   _____
   _____

3. _____
   _____
   _____
   _____

4. _____
   _____
   _____
   _____

© Pearson Education, Inc. All rights reserved.

Realidades **B**

Capítulo 5B

Nombre

Hora

Fecha

WRITING

Actividad 13

There is going to be a picnic at your new house, and your mother is telling you who is coming and what he or she will be bringing. Write what your mother says, using a name, a description word, and an item from the columns below. Use either **venir** or **traer** in your sentence. Use the names only once. Follow the model.

Nombre	Descripción	Va a traer
Los Sres. Vázquez	viejo	platos
	joven	tenedores
La Srta. Espinosa	contento	vasos
	simpático	pollo
Antonio Jerez	artístico	hamburguesas
	pelirrojo	pasteles
Fernando y María Sosa	enfermo	servilletas
	guapo	limonada
Catalina de la Cuesta	alto	cuchillos
	bajo	tazas

Modelo _La señorita Espinosa viene a la fiesta. Ella es la mujer joven y simpática que vive cerca de nuestra casa. Ella siempre está contenta y trae los pasteles._

1. _____

_____

2. _____

_____

3. _____

_____

4. _____

_____

© Pearson Education, Inc. All rights reserved.

VIDEO

Antes de ver el video

Actividad 1

Make a list of five items in your bedroom and five adjectives that describe your bedroom.

Cosas en mi dormitorio

_____

_____

_____

_____

_____

Descripción de mi dormitorio

_____

_____

_____

_____

_____

¿Comprendes?

Actividad 2

Below are some words and phrases that you have learned so far. On the lines below, write only the words that you most likely heard in the video episode about Ignacio's room.

a veces	ratón	bistec	¿A qué hora?	almuerzo
foto	desordenado	lámpara	pequeños	estante
pared	bueno	casa	mochila	peor
abuelos	bailar	cuarto	bicicleta	escritorio
calculadora	¿Adónde?	fiesta	discos compactos	color

_____ _____

_____ _____

_____ _____

_____ _____

_____ _____

© Pearson Education, Inc. All rights reserved.

Actividad 3

Put the following scenes from the video in chronological order by numbering them from 1–7.

_____

_____

_____

_____

_____

_____

_____

© Pearson Education, Inc. All rights reserved.

Y, ¿qué más?

Actividad 4

What is your room like? Is it messy or neat? What do you have to the left and to the right of the room? What do you have on the wall, on the nightstand, or on a bookshelf? Can you compare your room to someone else's? Describe your room, using as much new vocabulary as you can. Follow the sample paragraph below.

Modelo

Mi cuarto es menos ordenado que el cuarto de mi hermana. A la izquierda tengo un estante, muy desordenado, con discos compactos. A la derecha está mi escritorio con libros y revistas. Tengo una foto de mi familia en la pared. También tengo otra foto de mi hermana en su cuarto, ¡ y está ordenado!

_____

_____

_____

_____

_____

_____

© Pearson Education, Inc. All rights reserved.

Realidades B

Capítulo 6A

Nombre _____

Hora _____

Fecha _____

AUDIO

Actividad 5

Marta and her sister Ana have very similar bedrooms. However, since they have unique personalities and tastes, there are some differences! For each statement you hear, check off in the appropriate column whose bedroom is being described. You will hear each statement twice.

El dormitorio de Marta

El dormitorio de Ana

	Marta	Ana		Marta	Ana
1.	☐	☐	6.	☐	☐
2.	☐	☐	7.	☐	☐
3.	☐	☐	8.	☐	☐
4.	☐	☐	9.	☐	☐
5.	☐	☐	10.	☐	☐

© Pearson Education, Inc. All rights reserved.

Realidades **B**

Capítulo 6A

Nombre _____

Fecha _____

Hora _____

AUDIO

Actividad 6

Your Spanish teacher asks you to represent your school at a local university's **Competencia Escolar** (*Scholastic Competition*) for secondary Spanish students. She gives you a tape to practice with for the competition. As you listen to the recording, decide whether the statement is true or false and mark it in the grid. You will hear each set of statements twice.

	1	2	3	4	5	6	7	8	9	10
Cierto										
Falso										

Actividad 7

Sra. Harding's class is planning an Immersion Weekend for the school district's Spanish students. Listen as four committee members discuss the best food to have, the best activities for younger and older students, and the best colors for the t-shirt (**camiseta**) that will be given to all participants. To keep track of what everyone thinks, fill in the grid. You will hear each set of statements twice.

	La mejor comida	Las actividades para los estudiantes menores	Las actividades para los estudiantes mayores	El mejor color para la camiseta
1				
2				
3				
4				

© Pearson Education, Inc. All rights reserved.

Nombre _____ Hora _____

Fecha _____

Actividad 8

Your friend is babysitting for a family with an eight-year-old boy and a ten-year-old girl. Since they are a Spanish-speaking family, your friend wants you to go with her in case she doesn't understand everything that the mother tells her. Listen to the conversation to learn all the ground rules. Write either **sí** or **no** in each column that matches what the mother says that the boy or girl can do. Be sure to write **no** in both columns if neither is allowed to do it. Write **sí** in both columns if both are allowed to do it. You will hear this conversation twice.

© Pearson Education, Inc. All rights reserved.

Realidades B

Capítulo 6A

Nombre _____

Hora _____

Fecha _____

AUDIO

Actividad 9

Look at the pictures in the chart below as you hear people describe their friends' bedrooms. Place a check in the chart that corresponds to all of the items mentioned by the friend. You will hear each set of statements twice.

	Javier	Sara	María	Marcos

© Pearson Education, Inc. All rights reserved.

Realidades B

Capítulo 6A

Nombre _____

Hora _____

Fecha _____

WRITING

Actividad 10

Answer the following questions about your bedroom in complete sentences. If you prefer, you may write about your ideal bedroom.

1. ¿Cuál es tu color favorito?

   _____

2. ¿De qué color es tu dormitorio?

   _____

3. ¿Tienes una alfombra en tu dormitorio? ¿De qué color es?

   _____

4. ¿Tienes un despertador? ¿Cuándo usas tu despertador?

   _____

   _____

5. ¿Qué muebles (*furniture*) tienes en tu dormitorio?

   _____

   _____

6. ¿Qué cosas electrónicas tienes en tu dormitorio?

   _____

7. ¿Te gusta ver los DVDs? ¿Cuántos tienes?

   _____

8. ¿Cuántos discos compactos tienes?

   _____

© Pearson Education, Inc. All rights reserved.

Nombre _____   Hora _____

Fecha _____   **WRITING**

Actividad 11

A. Draw your bedroom or your ideal bedroom (including furniture, electronics, windows, books, decorations, and other possessions) in the space provided below.

 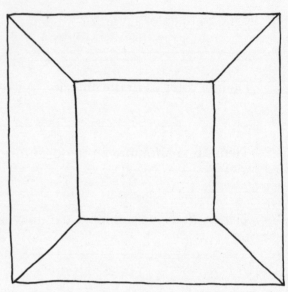

B. Now, compare the room that you drew with Juan's room on the left. Use the correct form of some of the following adjectives, or think of others: **práctico**, **interesante**, **grande**, **pequeño**, **mejor**, **peor**, **bonito**, **ordenado**.

| Modelo | *Mi dormitorio es menos interesante que el dormitorio de Juan.* |

1. _____

2. _____

3. _____

4. _____

5. _____

6. _____

© Pearson Education, Inc. All rights reserved.

Realidades Ⓑ

Capítulo 6A

Nombre _____

Hora _____

Fecha _____

WRITING

Actividad 12

You and your friends are comparing your English classes to determine which teacher's class to take next year. Read the information below, then compare the classes based on the criteria indicated. Follow the model.

	Clase A	Clase B	Clase C
Hora	Primera	Tercera	Octava
Profesor(a)	Profesora Brown — interesante	Profesor Martí — aburrido	Profesor Nicólas — muy interesante
Número de estudiantes	25	20	22
Dificultad	Difícil	Muy difícil	Fácil
Libros	Muy buenos	Aburridos	Buenos
Opinión general	A	B –	A –

Modelo Profesor *El profesor Martí es el menos interesante de los tres profesores.*

1. Hora (*temprano* or *tarde*)

_____

2. Número de estudiantes (*grande* or *pequeño)*

_____

3. Dificultad (*fácil* or *difícil*)

_____

4. Libros (*buenos* or *malos*)

_____

5. Opinión general (*mejor* or *peor*)

_____

_____

© Pearson Education, Inc. All rights reserved.

Nombre _____

Hora _____

Fecha _____

Actividad 13

Your parents are hosting a family reunion, and nine extra people will be sleeping at your house. On the lines below, write where nine guests would sleep at your house. You may use your imagination if you prefer.

1. _____

_____

2. _____

_____

3. _____

_____

4. _____

_____

5. _____

_____

6. _____

_____

7. _____

_____

8. _____

_____

9. _____

_____

© Pearson Education, Inc. All rights reserved.

Nombre _____

Hora _____

Fecha _____

VIDEO

Antes de ver el video

Actividad 1

Think of five chores you do at home. Then, write whether you like or don't like doing them using **me gusta** and **no me gusta nada**. Follow the model.

Modelo *No me gusta nada limpiar mi dormitorio.* _____

1. _____

2. _____

3. _____

4. _____

5. _____

¿Comprendes?

Actividad 2

As you know from the video, Jorgito does all of the chores even though some were Elena's responsibility. Next to each chore listed below, tell whether it was Elena's responsibility or Jorgito's responsibility by writing the appropriate name in the space provided.

1. _____ quitar el polvo

2. _____ poner la mesa del comedor

3. _____ lavar los platos en la cocina

4. _____ hacer la cama en el dormitorio de Jorge

5. _____ hacer la cama en el cuarto de Elena

6. _____ arreglar el dormitorio de Jorge

7. _____ pasar la aspiradora

8. _____ dar de comer al perro

© Pearson Education, Inc. All rights reserved.

VIDEO

Actividad 3

Use the stills below from the video to help you answer the questions. Use complete sentences.

¿A Elena le gusta trabajar en casa?

1. _____

¿Qué quiere Jorgito para ayudar a Elena?

2. _____

¿En qué están de acuerdo Elena y Jorgito?

_____

3. _____

¿Cuántos quehaceres le da Elena a Jorgito? ¿Por cuántas horas va a escuchar música Jorgito? _____

4. _____

Cuando vienen a casa, ¿cómo están los padres? _____

5. _____

En realidad, ¿es perezoso Jorgito?

6. _____

© Pearson Education, Inc. All rights reserved.

Y, ¿qué más?

Actividad 4

What activities might you do in each of these rooms? From the list in the box below, name at least two things that you might logically do in each room. Each activity should be used only once.

hacer la cama   pasar la aspiradora   escuchar música   cocinar la comida   poner la mesa   lavar los platos   quitar el polvo   comer la cena   arreglar el dormitorio desordenado   hacer la tarea

1. dormitorio de Elena

_____   _____

2. sala

_____   _____

3. comedor

_____   _____

4. cocina

_____   _____

5. dormitorio de Jorge

_____   _____

© Pearson Education, Inc. All rights reserved.

Realidades B

Capítulo 6B

Nombre _____

Hora _____

Fecha _____

AUDIO

Actividad 5

Listen as people look for things they have misplaced somewhere in their house. After each conversation, complete the sentence that explains what each person is looking for (**busca**) and in which room it is found. You will hear each dialogue twice.

1. La muchacha busca _____.

   Está en _____.

2. El muchacho busca _____.

   Está en _____.

3. La mujer busca _____.

   Está en _____.

4. El muchacho busca _____.

   Está en _____.

5. La muchacha busca _____.

   Está en _____.

Actividad 6

Señor Morales's nephew, Paco, volunteers to help his uncle move into a new apartment. However, Señor Morales is very distracted as he tells Paco where to put different things. Listen as he gives his nephew instructions and record in the grid below whether you think what he tells him to do each time is **lógico** (*logical*) **o ilógico** (*illogical*). You will hear each dialogue twice.

	1	2	3	4	5	6	7	8	9	10
lógico										
ilógico										

© Pearson Education, Inc. All rights reserved.

Realidades **B**

Capítulo 6B

Nombre _____

Hora _____

Fecha _____

AUDIO

Actividad 7

Nico's parents are shocked when they come home from a trip to find that he hasn't done any of the chores that he promised to do. As they tell Nico what he needs to do, fill in the blanks below each picture with the corresponding number. You will hear each set of statements twice.

_____   _____   _____   _____

_____   _____   _____

Actividad 8

Listen as each person rings a friend's doorbell and is told by the person who answers the door what the friend is doing at the moment. Based on that information, in which room of the house would you find the friend? As you listen to the conversations, look at the drawing of the house and write the number of the room that you think each friend might be in. You will hear each dialogue twice.

1. _____
2. _____
3. _____
4. _____
5. _____
6. _____

© Pearson Education, Inc. All rights reserved.

Nombre _____ Hora _____

Fecha _____ **AUDIO**

Actividad 9

Some people always seem to get out of doing their chores at home. Listen as a few teens tell their parents why they should not or cannot do what their parents have asked them to do. As you listen, write in the chart below what the parent requests, such as **lavar los platos**. Then write in the teens' excuses, such as **está lavando el coche**. You will hear each conversation twice.

	Los quehaceres	Las excusas
Marcos		
Luis		
Marisol		
Jorge		
Elisa		

© Pearson Education, Inc. All rights reserved.

Communication Workbook

Realidades **B**

Capítulo 6B

Nombre _____

Fecha _____

Hora _____

WRITING

Actividad 10

The Justino family is getting ready for their houseguests to arrive. Help Sra. Justino write the family's to-do list. Follow the model.

Modelo

En el dormitorio, tenemos que quitar el polvo, arreglar el cuarto y pasar la aspiradora.

1. _____
   _____
   _____

2. _____
   _____
   _____

3. _____
   _____
   _____

4. _____
   _____
   _____

© Pearson Education, Inc. All rights reserved.

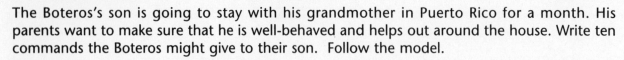

Realidades **B**

Capítulo 6B

Nombre

Hora

Fecha

WRITING

Actividad 11

The Boteros's son is going to stay with his grandmother in Puerto Rico for a month. His parents want to make sure that he is well-behaved and helps out around the house. Write ten commands the Boteros might give to their son. Follow the model.

Modelo   *Ayuda en la cocina, hijo.*

1. _____

2. _____

3. _____

4. _____

5. _____

6. _____

7. _____

8. _____

9. _____

10. _____

© Pearson Education, Inc. All rights reserved.

Nombre _____

Hora _____

Fecha _____

Actividad 12

The Galgo family is very busy on Sunday. Look at their schedule below and write what each family member is doing at the time given. Use your imagination, and use the model to help you.

	10:00	12:00	3:00	8:00
la Señora Galgo	hacer ejercicio	almorzar	trabajar	dormir
el Señor Galgo	trabajar	cortar el césped	preparar la cena	jugar al tenis
Rodrigo	arreglar el cuarto	comer	tocar la guitarra	estudiar
Mariana	nadar	poner la mesa	leer	ver la tele

Modelo 12:00 *A las doce, la Sra. Galgo está almorzando con sus amigos y el Sr. Galgo está cortando el césped. Rodrigo está comiendo una manzana y Mariana está poniendo la mesa.*

1. 10:00

_____

_____

_____

_____

2. 3:00

_____

_____

_____

_____

3. 8:00

_____

_____

_____

_____

© Pearson Education, Inc. All rights reserved.

WRITING

Actividad 13

A. Read the letter that Marta wrote to "Querida Adela," an advice column in the local paper, because she was frustrated with having to help around the house.

> Querida Adela:
>
> Yo soy una hija de 16 años y no tengo tiempo para ayudar en la casa. Mis padres no comprenden que yo tengo mi propia vida y que mis amigos son más importantes que los quehaceres de la casa. ¿Qué debo hacer?
>
> —Hija Malcontenta

B. Now, imagine that you are Adela and are writing a response to Marta. In the first paragraph, tell her what she must do around the house. In the second, tell her what she can do to still have fun with her friends. Use the sentences already below to help you.

Querida Hija Malcontenta:

Es verdad que tú tienes un problema. Piensas que tu vida con tus amigos es más importante que tu vida con tu familia. Pero, hija, tú tienes responsabilidades. Arregla tu cuarto. _____

_____

_____

Tienes que ser una buena hija.

Después de ayudar a tus padres, llama a tus amigos por teléfono.

_____

_____

_____. Tus padres van a estar más contentos y tú vas a tener una vida mejor.

Buena suerte

Adela

© Pearson Education, Inc. All rights reserved.

Realidades **B**

Capítulo 7A

Nombre _____

Fecha _____

Hora _____

VIDEO

Antes de ver el video

Actividad 1

In the next video, Claudia and Teresa go shopping for clothes. In order to make decisions on what they want they will sometimes make comparisons. Using the following words, make a comparative statement for each set. Follow the model.

Modelo   blusa roja / blusa amarilla

La blusa roja es más bonita que la blusa amarilla.

1. botas marrones / botas negras

_____

2. una falda larga / una mini falda

_____

3. un traje nuevo / un traje de moda (*in fashion*)

_____

4. Claudia – 16 años / Teresa – 15 años

_____

5. suéter que cuesta 40 dólares / suéter que cuesta 30 dólares

_____

¿Comprendes?

Actividad 2

Identify the speaker of the following quotes by writing the name of each person on the space provided.

1. "Tienes ropa muy bonita."   _____

2. "Quiero comprar algo nuevo."   _____

3.   "¿Qué tal esta tienda?"   _____

© Pearson Education, Inc. All rights reserved.

4. "Pues entonces, ¿esta falda y esta blusa?" _____

5. "Busco algo bonito para una fiesta." _____

6. "Bueno, hay cosas que no cuestan tanto." _____

7. "Bueno, uhm, aquí en México no llevamos
esa ropa en las fiestas." _____

8. "¡... pero es mi gorra favorita!" _____

Actividad 3

Can you remember what happened in the video? Write the letter of the correct answer on the line.

1. A Teresa no le gusta ni la falda ni el vestido; _____

   a. le quedan bien.

   b. le quedan más o menos.

   c. le quedan mal.

2. A Teresa no le gusta su ropa, pero sí tiene ropa _____

   a. bonita.

   b. fea.

   c. muy vieja.

3. Teresa quiere _____

   a. comprar algo extravagante.

   b. comprar algo nuevo.

   c. no ir a la fiesta.

© Pearson Education, Inc. All rights reserved.

Realidades **B**

Capítulo 7A

Nombre _____

Hora _____

Fecha _____

VIDEO

4. Claudia quiere ver _____

   a. cuánto cuestan la falda y la blusa.

   b. si le quedan bien los jeans y la camiseta.

   c. otras cosas más bonitas.

5. Por fin las chicas deciden comprar _____

   a. unos jeans de cuatrocientos pesos con una camiseta de doscientos pesos.

   b. en otra tienda.

   c. una falda de trescientos pesos y un suéter de doscientos pesos.

Y, ¿qué más?

Actividad 4

Do you like the clothes that you have in your closet? Write one sentence about something in your closet that you do like, and why. Then write one sentence about something in your closet that you don't like, and why not. Follow the models.

Modelo 1 _Me gusta el suéter negro porque es bonito y puedo llevarlo_

cuanto hace frío.

_____

_____

Modelo 2 _No me gustan los pantalones rojos porque son feos y me quedan mal._

_____

_____

© Pearson Education, Inc. All rights reserved.

Nombre _____ Hora _____

Fecha _____ **AUDIO**

Actividad 5

Isabel is working at a laundry (**lavandería**) in Salamanca. As the customers bring in their order, write how many clothing items each person has from each category in the appropriate boxes. Then total the order and write the amount in the blanks provided in the grid for each customer. You will hear each dialogue twice.

LAVANDERÍA DOS PASOS
(Note: € is the symbol for Euros)

	Precios	Cliente 1	Cliente 2	Cliente 3	Cliente 4	Cliente 5
Blusas	3 €					
Vestidos	6 €					
Pantalones	8 €					
Faldas	5 €					
Suéteres	5 €					
Camisas	3 €					
Jeans	7 €					
Chaquetas	9 €					
Camisetas	3 €					
	TOTAL	€	€	€	€	€

Actividad 6

Listen to the following items available from one of the shopping services on TV. You might not understand all of the words, but listen for the words that you do know in order to identify which item is being discussed. Then write down the price underneath the correct picture. You will hear each set of statements twice.

_____ _____ _____ _____ _____

© Pearson Education, Inc. All rights reserved.

Realidades **B**

Capítulo 7A

Nombre _____

Fecha _____

Hora _____

AUDIO

Actividad 7

Listen as friends talk about their plans for the weekend. Where are they thinking about going? What are they thinking about doing? How are they planning to dress? As you listen for these details, fill in the chart. You will hear each dialogue twice.

	¿Adónde piensa ir?	¿Qué piensa hacer?	¿Qué piensa llevar?
1. Paco			
2. Anita			
3. Ernesto			
4. Kiki			

Actividad 8

Susi is spending the summer in Ecuador, where she is living with a wonderful host family. As the summer comes to a close, she is searching for the perfect thank-you gifts for each member of the family. Listen as she talks to the sales clerk. In the chart below, write in the item that she decides to buy for each person in her new "family." You will hear this conversation twice.

Para la madre	Para el padre	Para el hijo, Luis	Para la hija, Marisol	Para el bebé

© Pearson Education, Inc. All rights reserved.

Nombre _____

Hora _____

Fecha _____

AUDIO

Actividad 9

What you wear can reveal secrets about your personality. Find out what type of message you send when you wear your favorite clothes and your favorite colors. As you listen to the descriptions, write down at least one word or phrase for each color personality and at least one article of clothing favored by that person. You will hear each set of statements twice.

EL COLOR	LA ROPA	LA PERSONALIDAD
Rojo		
Amarillo		
Morado		
Azul		
Anaranjado		
Marrón		
Gris		
Verde		
Negro		

© Pearson Education, Inc. All rights reserved.

Realidades Ⓑ

Capítulo 7A

Nombre _____

Hora _____

Fecha _____

WRITING

Actividad 10

Answer the following questions about clothing and shopping in complete sentences.

1. ¿Quién va mucho de compras en tu familia?

_____

2. ¿Piensas comprar ropa nueva esta estación? ¿Qué piensas comprar?

_____

_____

3. ¿Cuál prefieres, la ropa del verano o la ropa del invierno? ¿Por qué?

_____

_____

4. ¿Prefieres la ropa de tus amigos o la ropa de tus padres? ¿Por qué?

_____

_____

5. ¿Prefieres llevar ropa formal o informal?

_____

6. ¿Qué llevas normalmente para ir a la escuela?

_____

_____

7. ¿Cuál es tu ropa favorita? Describe.

_____

_____

_____

© Pearson Education, Inc. All rights reserved.

WRITING

Actividad 11

Some students are thinking about what to wear for the next school dance. Look at the pictures, then write complete sentences telling what the students might be thinking. Use the verbs **pensar, querer,** or **preferir.** Follow the model.

Modelo

María piensa llevar un vestido negro al baile. También quiere llevar
unos zapatos negros. Quiere ser muy elegante.

1. _____

_____

_____

2. _____

_____

_____

3. _____

_____

_____

© Pearson Education, Inc. All rights reserved.

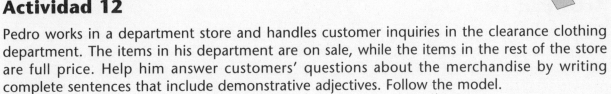

Realidades B

Capítulo 7A

Nombre _____

Fecha _____

Hora _____

WRITING

Actividad 12

Pedro works in a department store and handles customer inquiries in the clearance clothing department. The items in his department are on sale, while the items in the rest of the store are full price. Help him answer customers' questions about the merchandise by writing complete sentences that include demonstrative adjectives. Follow the model.

Modelo ¿Cuánto cuestan los suéteres?

Estos suéteres aquí cuestan cuarenta dólares y esos allí cuestan sesenta.

1. ¿Cuánto cuesta una gorra negra?

_____

2. ¿Cuánto cuestan los pantalones?

_____

3. ¿Las camisas cuestan diez dólares?

_____

4. ¿Cuánto cuesta un traje de baño?

_____

5. ¿Los jeans cuestan mucho?

_____

6. ¿La sudadera azul cuesta veinte dólares?

_____

7. ¿Cuánto cuestan las botas aquí?

_____

8. ¿Los abrigos cuestan mucho?

_____

© Pearson Education, Inc. All rights reserved.

WRITING

Actividad 13

You get a discount at the clothing store where you work after school, so you are going to buy presents for your friends and family there. Write complete sentences telling who you will buy gifts for and why you will choose each person's gift. Use the model to help you.

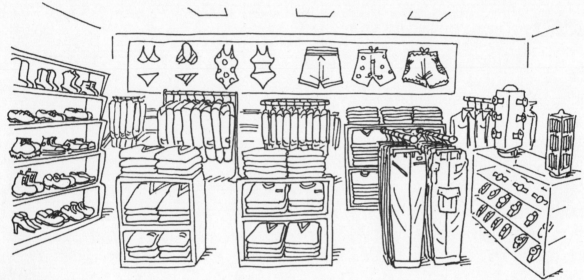

Modelo _Pienso comprar este suéter azul para mi madre porque ella prefiere la ropa del invierno._

1. _____

_____

2. _____

_____

3. _____

_____

4. _____

_____

5. _____

_____

© Pearson Education, Inc. All rights reserved.

VIDEO

Antes de ver el video

Actividad 1

Where do you like to shop? With a partner, write three things you like to buy and the best place to buy them.

Cosas para comprar

_____

_____

_____

Lugares donde comprarlas

_____

_____

_____

¿Comprendes?

Actividad 2

In the video, Claudia and Manolo go many places to find a gift for Manolo's aunt. Look at the places from the video below and number them in the order in which Manolo and Claudia pass them (from beginning to end).

_____  el almacén

_____  la joyería

_____ la tienda de software

_____  la parada de autobuses

_____ el centro comercial

© Pearson Education, Inc. All rights reserved.

VIDEO

Actividad 3

What happens when Claudia helps Manolo shop? Circle the letter of the correct answers.

1. Manolo necesita comprar un regalo para su tía porque

   a. mañana es su cumpleaños.

   b. mañana es su aniversario de bodas.

   c. mañana es su quinceañera.

2. El año pasado Manolo le compró a su tía

   a. unos aretes en la joyería.

   b. un libro en una librería.

   c. una corbata muy barata.

3. En el centro comercial, ellos ven

   a. videojuegos y software.

   b. pocas cosas en descuento.

   c. anteojos para sol, bolsos, carteras y llaveros.

4. Por fin, deciden comprar para la tía

   a. una cartera.

   b. un collar.

   c. un anillo.

5. Hay una confusión y Manolo le regala a la tía

   a. una pulsera.

   b. unos guantes.

   c. un collar de perro.

© Pearson Education, Inc. All rights reserved.

Communication Workbook

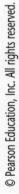

Y, ¿qué más?

Actividad 4

You are shopping for a birthday gift for your mother. Fill in the dialogue below with your possible responses.

DEPENDIENTE: ¿Qué desea usted?

TÚ: _____

_____

DEPENDIENTE: ¿Prefiere ver ropa, perfumes o joyas para ella?

TÚ: _____

_____

DEPENDIENTE: Aquí hay muchos artículos, pero no cuestan tanto.

TÚ: _____

_____

© Pearson Education, Inc. All rights reserved.

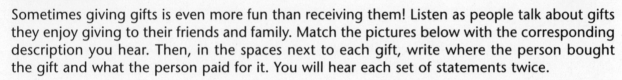

Realidades B

Capítulo 7B

Nombre _____

Hora _____

Fecha _____

AUDIO

Actividad 5

Sometimes giving gifts is even more fun than receiving them! Listen as people talk about gifts they enjoy giving to their friends and family. Match the pictures below with the corresponding description you hear. Then, in the spaces next to each gift, write where the person bought the gift and what the person paid for it. You will hear each set of statements twice.

	Descripción	Lugar de compra	Precio
1.	_____	_____	_____
2.	_____	_____	_____
3.	_____	_____	_____
4.	_____	_____	_____
5.	_____	_____	_____

Actividad 6

Listen to the following mini-conversations about different kinds of stores. Circle **lógico** if the conversation makes sense and **ilógico** if it does not. You will hear each dialogue twice.

1. lógico   ilógico
2. lógico   ilógico
3. lógico   ilógico
4. lógico   ilógico
5. lógico   ilógico

6. lógico   ilógico
7. lógico   ilógico
8. lógico   ilógico
9. lógico   ilógico
10. lógico   ilógico

© Pearson Education, Inc. All rights reserved.

Realidades B

Capítulo 7B

Nombre _____

Hora _____

Fecha _____

AUDIO

Actividad 7

Listen as Lorena shows a friend her photographs. Write a sentence describing each one as you hear Lorena describe it. You will hear each conversation twice.

1. Lorena _____ hace _____.

2. Lorena _____ hace _____.

3. Lorena _____ hace _____.

4. Lorena _____ hace _____.

5. Lorena _____ hace _____.

Actividad 8

You have been waiting in line all day at the mall, so you have overheard many conversations as you waited. See if you can match each conversation with the illustrations below and write the number of each conversation under the correct illustration. You will hear each conversation twice.

_____ _____ _____ _____

© Pearson Education, Inc. All rights reserved.

AUDIO

Actividad 9

As a special holiday service, **El Almacén Continental** is sponsoring a hotline that customers can call to get gift ideas. Listen as callers tell the store specialist what they have bought for a particular person in the past. Then listen to the specialist's suggestion for this year's gift. Use the chart below to take notes. You will hear each conversation twice.

	La personalidad y las actividades de la persona	El regalo del año pasado	¿Un regalo para este año?
1			
2			
3			
4			
5			

© Pearson Education, Inc. All rights reserved.

Realidades Ⓑ

Capítulo 7B

Nombre _____

Fecha _____

Hora _____

WRITING

Actividad 10

You are talking to a friend about what you buy when you go shopping. Tell what items you usually buy in each of the specialty shops suggested by the pictures. Then, tell what other items are available at the store. Use the model to help you.

Modelo

En la zapatería, compro zapatos y botas. También es posible comprar
guantes y carteras en una zapatería.

1. _____

_____

_____

2. _____

_____

_____

3. _____

_____

_____

© Pearson Education, Inc. All rights reserved.

Realidades B

Capítulo 7B

Nombre _____

Fecha _____

Hora _____

WRITING

Actividad 11

In your Spanish class, you are asked to learn the dates of some important events in the history and culture of Spanish-speaking countries. To help you memorize these dates, write sentences telling when each event occurred. Follow the model.

Modelo   Pablo Picasso / pintar su cuadro *Guernica* / 1937

_*Pablo Picasso pintó su cuadro **Guernica** en 1937.*_____

1. Los Estados Unidos / declarar su independencia / el cuatro de julio, 1776

_____

2. Vicente Fox / ganar la presidencia de México / 2000

_____

3. Antonio Banderas / actuar en la película *The Mambo Kings* / 1993

_____

4. Los jugadores argentinos / ganar la Copa Mundial (*World Cup*) / 1986

_____

5. Yo / comprar mis primeros zapatos / ???

_____

6. Nosotros / entrar en la clase de español / ???

_____

7. Los Juegos Olímpicos / pasar en España / 1992

_____

8. México / declarar su independencia / el quince de septiembre, 1810

_____

9. Simón Bolívar / liberar a Venezuela / 1821

_____

© Pearson Education, Inc. All rights reserved.

Realidades **B**

Capítulo 7B

Nombre _____

Hora _____

Fecha _____

WRITING

Actividad 12

The people in your neighborhood were very busy yesterday. Write at least three sentences about what they all did based on the pictures, using at least one of these verbs: **buscar, jugar, pagar, practicar, sacar, tocar.** Follow the model.

Modelo El Sr. Rodríguez

Ayer el Sr. Rodríguez enseñó la clase de español. La clase practicó la lección. Los estudiantes usaron las computadoras para hacer las actividades.

1. Andrés

_____

_____

_____

2. yo

_____

_____

_____

3. yo   mi madre

_____

_____

© Pearson Education, Inc. All rights reserved.

4. tú

_____

_____

_____

5. Juana e Inés

_____

_____

_____

Actividad 13

You are writing a letter to your aunt in Mexico to tell her what you bought for your family for the holidays. In the letter, tell what you bought for each person, in what stores you found the items, and how much you paid. The letter has been started for you.

Querida Tía:

Saludos de los Estados Unidos. Te escribo para decirte que terminé de comprar los

regalos para la familia. Para _____ , compré un suéter bonito. ¡Lo encontré en

el almacén por sólo veinte dólares! _____

_____

_____

_____

Bueno, nos vemos en una semana. ¡Buena suerte con las compras!

Un fuerte abrazo,

Tu sobrino(a) _____

© Pearson Education, Inc. All rights reserved.

Realidades B

Capítulo 8A

Nombre _____

Fecha _____

Hora _____

VIDEO

Antes de ver el video

Actividad 1

You can see and learn a lot on a day trip. Make a list of four places you would like to visit for the day, and write next to each one the main attraction that you would like to see there. Follow the model.

Lugares	Cosas que ver
Modelo *Granada, España*	*La Alhambra*
_____	_____
_____	_____
_____	_____
_____	_____

¿Comprendes?

Actividad 2

Raúl, Gloria, and Tomás went on a day trip to San José and Sarapiquí Park. Under each heading, write the things that they saw in San José and the things that they saw in Sarapiquí Park.

Ministerio de Cultura	mono	Parque España	Catarata La Paz
Gran Terminal del Caribe	palma	bosque lluvioso	Teatro Nacional

San José	Parque Sarapiquí
_____	_____
_____	_____
_____	_____
_____	_____

© Pearson Education, Inc. All rights reserved.

VIDEO

Actividad 3

Based on the video story that you just watched, circle the most appropriate word to complete each statement.

1. Raúl, Gloria y Tomás salieron de la casa muy (tarde / temprano) para ir al parque Sarapiquí.

2. Para ir al parque ellos tomaron el (autobús / avión).

3. El viaje dura (una hora y media / dos horas), porque el parque está a 82 (kilómetros / millas) de San José.

4. En el parque (hace mucho calor / no hace ni frío ni calor) pero llueve mucho.

5. Raúl compra los (libros / boletos) en la Estación Biológica La Selva y cuestan 3,600 (pesos / colones).

6. Tomás tiene la (mochila / cámara) y el (boleto / mapa) y está listo para explorar el parque.

7. Ellos tienen mucho cuidado cuando caminan, pues las raíces de los árboles son muy (grandes / interesantes).

8. Gloria le dice a Tomás: "Hay más de cuatrocientas especies de (monos / aves) en el parque."

9. Ellos tienen problemas al (sacar las fotos / regresar a casa). Pero Tomás (quiere / no quiere) continuar.

10. Raúl dice: "Fue un día (interesante / desastre) pero un poco (difícil / aburrido) para Tomás."

© Pearson Education, Inc. All rights reserved.

Realidades B

Capítulo 8A

Nombre _____

Hora _____

Fecha _____

VIDEO

Y, ¿qué más?

Actividad 4

Based on what you learned in the video, imagine that you took a field trip to Costa Rica. Your best friend is curious about your trip. Answer your friend's questions below.

1. —¿Cómo es el parque Sarapiquí?

   _____

2. —¿Sacaste fotos del parque?

   _____

3. —¿Qué fue lo que más te gustó?

   _____

4. —¿Qué fue lo que menos te gustó?

   _____

5. —¿Cuál es la comida típica de Costa Rica?

   _____

© Pearson Education, Inc. All rights reserved.

Nombre _____ Hora _____

Fecha _____

AUDIO

Actividad 5

You call a toll-free telephone number in order to qualify for the popular radio game show, **"Palabras Secretas"** (*Secret Words*). Your challenge is to guess each secret word within ten seconds. Listen to the clues and try to guess the word as the clock is ticking. You must write your answer down before the buzzer in order to be ready for the next one. You will hear each set of statements twice.

1. _____ 5. _____

2. _____ 6. _____

3. _____ 7. _____

4. _____ 8. _____

Actividad 6

Listen as a husband and wife talk to a travel agent about their upcoming vacation. Where would each like to go? What type of things would each like to do? Most importantly, do they agree on what is the ideal trip? As you listen, write as much information as you can in each person's travel profile in the chart below. Can you think of a place they could go where both of them would be happy? You will hear this conversation twice.

	EL SEÑOR	LA SEÑORA
¿Adónde le gustaría ir?		
¿Por qué le gustaría ir a ese lugar?		
Cuando va de vacaciones, ¿qué le gustaría hacer?	1. 2.	1. 2.
¿Qué le gustaría ver?	1. 2.	1. 2.
¿Cómo le gustaría viajar?		
¿Adónde deben ir?		

© Pearson Education, Inc. All rights reserved.

Communication Workbook

Realidades B

Capítulo 8A

Nombre _____

Hora _____

Fecha _____

AUDIO

Actividad 7

Listen as mothers call their teenaged sons and daughters on their cell phones to see if they have done what they were asked to do. Based on what each teenager says, categorize the answers in the chart. You will hear each conversation twice.

	1	2	3	4	5	6	7	8	9	10
Teen did what the parent asked him or her to do.										
Teen is in the middle of doing what the parent asked him or her to do.										
Teen says he/she is going to do what the parent asked him/her to do.										

Actividad 8

Your Spanish teacher has asked the students in your class to survey each other about a topic of interest. In order to give you a model to follow, your teacher will play a recording of part of a student's survey from last year. Listen to the student's questions, and fill in his survey form. You will hear each conversation twice.

	¿EL LUGAR?
1. Marco	
2. Patricia	
3. Chucho	
4. Rita	
5. Margarita	

© Pearson Education, Inc. All rights reserved.

Actividad 9

Everyone loves a superhero, and the listeners of this Hispanic radio station are no exception. Listen to today's episode of "Super Tigre," as the hero helps his friends try to locate the evil Rona Robles! Super Tigre tracks Rona Robles down by asking people when they last saw her and where she went. Keep track of what the people said by filling in the chart. You will hear each conversation twice.

	¿Dónde la vio?	¿A qué hora la vio?	¿Qué hizo ella? *(What did she do?)*	¿Adónde fue ella?
1				
2				
3				
4				
5				

Where did Super Tigre finally find Rona Robles? _____

© Pearson Education, Inc. All rights reserved.

WRITING

Actividad 10

Answer the following questions in complete sentences.

1. ¿Te gusta ir de viaje? ¿Te gustaría más ir de vacaciones al campo o a una ciudad?

   _____

   _____

2. ¿Visitaste algún parque nacional en el pasado? ¿Cuál(es)? Si no, ¿te gustaría visitar

   un parque nacional? _____

   _____

3. ¿Vives cerca de un lago? ¿Cómo se llama? ¿Te gusta nadar? ¿Pasear en bote?

   _____

   _____

4. ¿Te gusta ir al mar? ¿Qué te gusta hacer allí? Si no, ¿por qué no? _____

   _____

   _____

5. ¿Montaste a caballo alguna vez? ¿Te gustó o no? Si no, ¿te gustaría montar a caballo?

   _____

   _____

6. Describe tu lugar favorito para vivir. ¿Está cerca de un lago? ¿Cerca o lejos de
   la ciudad? ¿Hay montañas / museos / parques / un mar cerca de tu casa ideal?

   _____

   _____

   _____

© Pearson Education, Inc. All rights reserved.

Nombre _____ Hora _____

Fecha _____ **WRITING**

Actividad 11

You and your friends are talking about what you did over the weekend. Write complete sentences based on the illustrations to tell what the following people did. Follow the model.

Modelo Pablo _vio una película_ _____.

1. Mariela y su madre _____.

2. Nosotros _____.

3. Yo _____.

4. Roberto _____.

5. Norma _____.

6. Tú _____.

7. Ignacio e Isabel _____.

© Pearson Education, Inc. All rights reserved.

Actividad 12

You and your friends were very busy yesterday. Tell all the places where each person went using the illustrations as clues. Follow the model.

Modelo   Melisa y su padre *fueron de compras.* _____

Después, fueron al cine. _____

1.   David _____

_____

_____

2.   Yo _____

_____

_____

3.   Nosotros _____

_____

_____

4.   Raquel y Tito _____

_____

_____

© Pearson Education, Inc. All rights reserved.

Nombre _____

Hora _____

Fecha _____

WRITING

Actividad 13

A. Write two sentences telling what places you visited the last time you went on vacation. You can write about your ideal vacation if you would prefer. Follow the model.

Modelo *Fui al parque de diversiones.* _____

1. _____

2. _____

B. Write two sentences telling about people you saw when you were on vacation.

Modelo *Vi a mi abuela.* _____

1. _____

2. _____

C. Now, complete the letter below to your friend. Use your sentences from Part A and Part B and additional details to tell him or her about your vacation.

Querido(a) _____ :

¡Hola! ¿Cómo estás? Gracias por tu carta de la semana pasada. Te voy a contar un

poco de nuestras vacaciones del mes pasado. _____

_____

_____

_____

Y cuando fuimos a otro lugar, vimos _____

_____

_____

_____

_____

_____

Un abrazo,

_____

Communication Workbook

© Pearson Education, Inc. All rights reserved.

Nombre _____   Hora _____

Fecha _____

VIDEO

Antes de ver el video

Actividad 1

There are lots of things you can do to make the world a better place. Under each category, write two things that you would like to do to help.

Cómo ayudar...

en mi comunidad _____

_____

con el ambiente _____

_____

¿Comprendes?

Actividad 2

In the video, the friends talk about how to help in their communities through volunteer work. Circle the letter of the appropriate answer for each question.

1. Gloria y Raúl trabajan como voluntarios en

   a. un centro de ancianos.

   b. Casa Latina.

   c. el Hospital Nacional de Niños.

2. Tomás va al hospital porque

   a. está enfermo.

   b. a él le encanta el trabajo voluntario.

   c. tiene que llevar ropa para los niños.

3. Gloria dice: "Trabajar con los niños en el hospital es

   a. muy aburrido."

   b. una experiencia inolvidable."

   c. un trabajo que no me gusta."

© Pearson Education, Inc. All rights reserved.

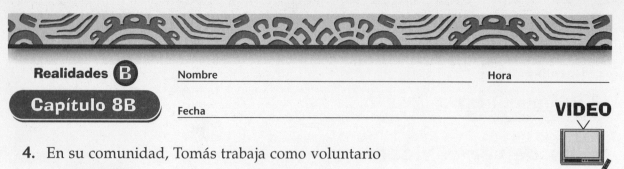

VIDEO

4. En su comunidad, Tomás trabaja como voluntario

    a. dando comida a los pobres.

    b. enseñando a leer a los ancianos.

    c. recogiendo ropa usada para los pobres.

5. Ellos también cuidan el ambiente reciclando

    a. aluminio y periódicos.

    b. papel, plástico y vidrio.

    c. papel, vidrio y aluminio.

Actividad 3

Fill in the blanks from the box below to complete the story.

reciclar	importante	libros	pasado
ancianos	comunidad	voluntarios	difícil
lava	simpáticos	trabajo	

En el Hospital Nacional de Niños, Tomás y Gloria trabajan como (1) _____ .

Allí ellos cantan, leen (2) _____ y juegan con los niños. A veces los niños

están muy enfermos y es (3) _____ , pero los niños son muy

(4) _____ . Raúl trabajó en un centro de (5) _____ el año (6)

_____ . Allí les ayudó con la comida y hablando con ellos.

   Tomás también trabaja en su (7) _____ ; él ayuda a recoger ropa usada.

Después la separa, la (8) _____ y luego la da a la gente pobre del barrio.

Es mucho (9) _____ , pero le gusta.

   Todos ellos ayudan a (10) _____ el papel y las botellas pues, piensan que

reciclar y conservar es muy (11) _____ .

© Pearson Education, Inc. All rights reserved.

Realidades **B**

Capítulo 8B

Nombre _____

Hora _____

Fecha _____

VIDEO

Y, ¿qué más?

Actividad 4

Now that you have seen Tomás, Gloria, and Raúl working in various ways to help others, think about the organizations that make it possible for them to do this work. Imagine that you work with one of the organizations listed below, and write a paragraph about your experiences. Use the model to help you.

el Hospital Nacional de Niños

un centro de ancianos

el club Casa Latina

Modelo   *Me gusta trabajar en el centro de ancianos. Les ayudo con la*
          comida y paso tiempo escuchando sus cuentos.

_____

_____

_____

_____

_____

_____

© Pearson Education, Inc. All rights reserved.

Actividad 5

Listen as Sra. Muñoz, the Spanish Club sponsor, asks several students what they did last weekend. If a student's actions had a positive impact on their community, place a check mark in the corresponding box or boxes. If a student's actions had no positive effect on their community, place an X in the corresponding box or boxes. You will hear each conversation twice.

	Javier	Ana	José	Celi	Pablo	Laura	Sra. Muñoz
enseñar a los niños a leer							
reciclar la basura de las calles							
jugar al fútbol con amigos							
recoger y lavar la ropa usada para la gente pobre							
trabajar en un centro para ancianos							
traer juguetes a los niños que están en el hospital							
trabajar en un restaurante del centro comercial							

Actividad 6

Listen as people talk about what they did last Saturday. Did they do volunteer work in the community or did they earn spending money for themselves? Place a check mark in the correct box on the grid. You will hear each set of statements twice.

	1	2	3	4	5	6	7	8

© Pearson Education, Inc. All rights reserved.

Nombre _____   Hora _____

Fecha _____   **AUDIO**

Actividad 7

Listen as our leaders, friends, and family give advice to teenagers about what we must do to serve our communities. Use the grid below to take notes as you listen. Then, use your notes to complete the sentences below. For example, you might write "**El vicepresidente de los Estados Unidos** *dice que hay que reciclar la basura de las calles.*" In the last sentence, complete a statement about your personal suggestion for others. You will hear each set of statements twice.

¿Quién(es) lo dice(n)?	¿Qué dice(n)?
1. El presidente de los Estados Unidos	
2. Mis padres	
3. Los médicos del hospital	
4. Mis profesores	
5. Mis amigos y yo	

1. El presidente de los Estados Unidos _____

_____ .

2. Los padres _____

_____ .

3. Los médicos _____

_____ .

4. Los profesores _____

_____ .

5. Mis amigos _____

_____ .

6. Yo _____

© Pearson Education, Inc. All rights reserved.

Actividad 8

As you hear each of the following statements, imagine whom the speaker might be addressing. Choose from the list of people, and write the number of the statement on the corresponding blank. You will hear each set of statements twice.

_____ al médico   _____ a sus padres

_____ a la policía   _____ a un niño de cinco años

_____ al camarero   _____ a un voluntario del hospital

_____ a la profesora de español _____ a una persona que trabaja en el zoológico

Actividad 9

Abuela Consuelo always has her grandchildren over for the holidays. She wants to know what they have done over the past year. They also remind her what she gave them last year as a gift. Use the grid to help keep track of each grandchild's story. You will hear each conversation twice.

	¿Qué hizo el niño el año pasado?	¿Qué le dio la abuela al niño el año pasado?
Marta		
Jorge		
Sara		
Miguel		
Angélica		

© Pearson Education, Inc. All rights reserved.

Communication Workbook

Realidades ❶

Capítulo 8B

Nombre _____

Fecha _____

Hora _____

WRITING

Actividad 10

Answer the following questions in complete sentences.

1. ¿Hay lugares para hacer trabajo voluntario en tu comunidad?

_____

¿Qué hacen allí? _____

_____

2. ¿Te gustaría trabajar como voluntario en:

un hospital? ¿Por qué? _____

_____

un centro para personas pobres? ¿Por qué? _____

_____

un centro para ancianos? ¿Por qué? _____

_____

3. ¿Tu familia recicla? _____

¿Qué reciclan Uds.? _____

_____

¿Por qué es importante reciclar? _____

_____

¿Te gustaría ayudar con el reciclaje en tu comunidad? _____

_____

© Pearson Education, Inc. All rights reserved.

Nombre _____ Hora _____

Fecha _____

Actividad 11

All of the following people were asked to speak on a subject. You are reporting on what everyone says. Use each item only once. Follow the model.

yo	el trabajo voluntario
nosotros	el campamento de deportes
Sra. Ayala	el reciclaje
Dr. Riviera	el fútbol
tú	el teatro
Paco	la ropa
José y María	la salud
Alicia y yo	los quehaceres

Modelo   *La señora Ayala dice que el trabajo voluntario es una*
experiencia inolvidable.

1. _____

2. _____

3. _____

4. _____

5. _____

6. _____

7. _____

© Pearson Education, Inc. All rights reserved.

Actividad 12

You are finding out what everyone's plans are for the weekend. Choose a verb and a direct object pronoun from the banks and write a sentence about weekend plans for each subject given. Use each verb only once. Follow the model.

ayudar	dar	decir	enseñar	escribir
hacer	invitar	leer	llevar	traer

me	te	le	nos	les

Modelo *Miguel y Elena nos invitan a su fiesta.*

1. Mis padres _____.

2. Yo _____.

3. Uds. _____.

4. Nuestra profesora de español _____.

5. El presidente _____.

6. Rafael y Gabriel _____.

7. Tu mejor amigo _____.

8. El Sr. Fuentes _____.

9. La Sra. Allende _____.

10. Tú _____.

© Pearson Education, Inc. All rights reserved.

Realidades **B**

Capítulo 8B

Nombre

Fecha

Hora

WRITING

Actividad 13

Last week, your Spanish class did some volunteer work at the local nursing home. Read the thank you letter from the residents, then write a paragraph explaining at least four things that you and your classmates did for them. Remember to use the preterite tense and indirect object pronouns where necessary. Follow the model.

> Queridos muchachos:
>
> Les escribimos para decirles "gracias" por su generosa visita de la semana pasada.
> A la señora Blanco le gustó el libro de poesía que Uds. le regalaron. Todos lo pasamos bien. Nos gustó especialmente la canción "Feliz Navidad" que cantó Luisita. El señor Marcos todavía habla de los pasteles que las chicas le trajeron. Y nuestro jardín está más bonito que nunca, después de todo su trabajo. En fin, mil gracias de parte de todos aquí en Pinos Sombreados. Esperamos verles pronto.
>
> Fuertes abrazos,
> Los residentes

Modelo _Nosotros visitamos a los residentes de Pinos Sombreados la semana pasada._

_____

_____

_____

_____

_____

_____

_____

_____

© Pearson Education, Inc. All rights reserved.

Nombre _____

Hora _____

Fecha _____

VIDEO

Antes de ver el video

Actividad 1

In the second column, write the title of a movie or a television program that is associated with the category in the first column. The first one is done for you.

Programa o película	Nombre del programa o película
telenovelas	"Days of Our Lives"
noticias	
programas de entrevistas	
programas de la vida real	
películas de ciencia ficción	
programas de concurso	
programas educativos	
programas de deportes	
comedias	
dibujos animados	
películas románticas	
programas infantiles	

© Pearson Education, Inc. All rights reserved.

Realidades **B**

Capítulo 9A

Nombre _____

Hora _____

Fecha _____

VIDEO

¿Comprendes?

Actividad 2

Look at the pictures and write what type of program each one is. Then, write the name of the character in the video who likes this type of program.

	CATEGORY	CHARACTER'S NAME
1.	_____	_____
2.	_____	_____
3.	_____	_____
4.	_____	_____
5.	_____	_____

Actividad 3

Using complete sentences, answer the following questions about what happens in the video.

1. ¿Quién tiene el mando a distancia primero?

_____

2. ¿Qué piensa Ana de la telenovela "El amor es loco"?

_____

© Pearson Education, Inc. All rights reserved.

Realidades **B**

Capítulo 9A

Nombre

Hora

Fecha

VIDEO

3. ¿A quiénes les encantan las telenovelas?

_____

4. ¿Qué piensa Ignacio de los programas de la vida real?

_____

5. ¿Qué piensa Jorgito de escuchar música en el cuarto de su hermana?

_____

6. ¿Qué deciden hacer los amigos al final?

_____

7. ¿Qué quiere ver Elena en el cine? ¿Están de acuerdo Ignacio y Javier?

_____

Y, ¿qué más?

Actividad 4

What kind of TV programs do you like? What type of movies do you enjoy watching? Explain your preferences. Follow the model.

Modelo

A mí me gustan mucho los programas de concursos; son muy divertidos porque puedes jugarlos en casa con tu familia o amigos. Mi hermano prefiere los deportes; siempre quiere el mando a distancia para ver los juegos. Cuando voy al cine prefiero ver comedias, pues las películas románticas son aburridas.

_____

_____

_____

_____

© Pearson Education, Inc. All rights reserved.

Realidades Ⓑ

Capítulo 9A

Nombre _____

Hora _____

Fecha _____

AUDIO

Actividad 5

Your friend is reading you the television line-up for a local television station. After listening to each program description, fill in on the grid what day or days the program is shown, what time it is shown, and what type of program it is. You will hear each set of statements twice.

	Día(s)	Hora	Clase de programa
"Mi computadora"			
"La detective Morales"			
"Cine en su sofá"			
"Las aventuras del Gato Félix"			
"Cara a cara"			
"Lo mejor del béisbol"			
"Marisol"			
"Festival"			
"Treinta minutos"			
"Las Américas"			

Actividad 6

Listen as people in a video rental store talk about what kind of movie they want to rent. After listening to each conversation, put the letter of the type of film they agree on in the space provided. You will hear each conversation twice.

1. _____   A. una película policíaca

2. _____   B. una comedia

3. _____   C. un drama

4. _____   D. una película de ciencia ficción

5. _____   E. una película romántica

6. _____   F. una película de horror

7. _____   G. una película de dibujos animados

© Pearson Education, Inc. All rights reserved.

Communication Workbook

Realidades B

Capítulo 9A

Nombre _____

Hora _____

Fecha _____

AUDIO

Actividad 7

Listen to a film critic interviewing five people on opening night of the movie *Marruecos*. After listening to each person's interview, circle the number of stars that closely matches the person's opinion of the movie, from a low rating of one star to a high rating of four. After noting all of the opinions, give the movie an overall rating of one to four stars, and give a reason for your answer. You will hear each conversation twice.

	No le gustó nada	Le gustó más o menos	Le gustó mucho	Le encantó
1.	[★]	[★★]	[★★★]	[★★★★]
2.	[★]	[★★]	[★★★]	[★★★★]
3.	[★]	[★★]	[★★★]	[★★★★]
4.	[★]	[★★]	[★★★]	[★★★★]
5.	[★]	[★★]	[★★★]	[★★★★]

¿Cuántas estrellas para *Marruecos*? ¿Por qué? _____

_____

Actividad 8

Listen as two friends talk on the phone about what they just saw on TV. Do they seem to like the same type of programs? As you listen to their conversation, fill in the Venn diagram, indicating: 1) which programs only Alicia likes; 2) which programs both Alicia and Laura like; and 3) which programs only Laura likes. You will hear this conversation twice.

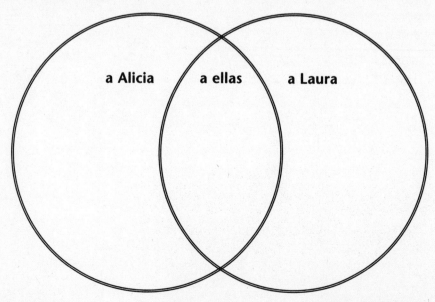

a Alicia   a ellas   a Laura

© Pearson Education, Inc. All rights reserved.

Nombre

Hora

Fecha

AUDIO

Actividad 9

Listen as a television critic reviews some of the new shows of the season. As you listen, determine which shows he likes and dislikes, and why. Fill in the chart. You will hear each paragraph twice.

	Le gusta...	¿Por qué le gusta?	No le gusta...	¿Por qué no le gusta?
1				
2				
3				
4				
5				

© Pearson Education, Inc. All rights reserved.

Actividad 10

Answer the following questions about movies and television.

1. ¿Te gusta ir al cine?

_____

2. ¿Prefieres los dramas o las comedias? ¿Por qué? _____

_____

3. ¿Cómo se llama tu película favorita? ¿Qué clase de película es?

_____

_____

4. ¿Te gustan las películas policíacas? ¿Por qué? _____

_____

5. ¿Te gusta más ver le tele o leer? ¿Por qué? _____

_____

_____

6. ¿Qué clase de programas prefieres? ¿Por qué? _____

_____

_____

7. ¿Cuántos canales de televisión puedes ver en casa? _____

¿Cuál es tu canal favorito? _____

¿Por qué? _____

8. ¿Tienes un programa favorito? ¿Cómo se llama? _____

_____

© Pearson Education, Inc. All rights reserved.

Nombre _____

Hora _____

Fecha _____

WRITING

Actividad 11

Your school newspaper printed a picture of the preparations for the Cinco de Mayo party at your school. Describe the photo using a form of **acabar de** + infinitive to tell what everyone just finished doing before the picture was taken.

Ramón   Julia   Ana   Sra. Lemaños   Yo   Isabel

Modelo   *Horacio Ibáñez acaba de sacar la foto.* _____

1. Isabel _____

_____

2. Julia y Ramón _____

_____

3. Yo _____

_____

4. La señora Lemaños _____

_____

5. Ana _____

_____

© Pearson Education, Inc. All rights reserved.

Actividad 12

You and your friends are talking about movies. Tell about people's preferences by choosing a subject from the first column and matching it with words from the other two columns to make complete sentences. Use each subject only once, but words from the other columns can be used more than once. Follow the model.

nosotros	gustar	las películas románticas
mis padres	encantar	las película de horror
mí	aburrir	las películas policíacas
ti	interesar	las comedias
los profesores	disgustar	los dramas
mis amigas		
mi abuelo		

Modelo   *A mí me encantan las películas románticas.* _____

1. _____

2. _____

3. _____

4. _____

5. _____

6. _____

© Pearson Education, Inc. All rights reserved.

Nombre _____ Hora _____

Fecha _____

WRITING

Actividad 13

You are writing your new Spanish-speaking pen pal an e-mail about American television. First tell him about a program that you just saw. What type of show was it? Did you like it? Was it interesting? Then, tell him about two other types of TV shows that are popular in America. Make sure to tell him your opinion of these types of shows, and what some other people you know think about them.

Fecha: 20 de abril

Tema: La televisión

Querido Pancho:

¡Hola! ¿Cómo estás? Acabo de terminar de ver el programa _____

_____ . A mí _____

_____

_____

_____

En los Estados Unidos, la gente ve mucho la tele. _____

_____

_____

_____

_____

_____

¡Te escribo pronto!

Un abrazo,

_____

© Pearson Education, Inc. All rights reserved.

Realidades Ⓑ

Capítulo 9B

Nombre _____

Hora _____

Fecha _____

VIDEO

Antes de ver el video

Actividad 1

How do you communicate with your friends from far away? Using the word bank below, write two sentences about how you might stay in touch with long distance friends.

cámara digital	correo electrónico
ordenador / computadora	cibercafé
navegar en la Red	página Web
información	salones de chat
dirección electrónica	foto digital

_____

_____

_____

_____

¿Comprendes?

Actividad 2

Javier is becoming accustomed to living in Spain, but he has a lot to learn about technology. What does Ana teach him? Write **cierto** (*true*) or **falso** (*false*) next to each statement.

1. Javier conoce muy bien las cámaras digitales. _____

2. Él va a enviar una tarjeta a su amigo Esteban. _____

3. Javier le saca una foto de Ana y le gusta la cámara. _____

4. Él piensa que no es muy complicada la cámara digital. _____

5. Ana lo lleva a un cibercafé, para ordenar un café. _____

6. Empiezan a navegar en la Red. _____

7. Ana busca su página Web, pero Javier no la quiere ver. _____

8. No hay mucha información en la Red. _____

© Pearson Education, Inc. All rights reserved.

9. Pueden visitar los salones de chat, pero
   prefieren escribirle un correo electrónico a Esteban. _____

10. Esteban ve la foto digital de su amigo y piensa que está triste. _____

Actividad 3

Complete the sentences below with information from the video.

1. Javier va a enviar _____ a
   su amigo Esteban.

2. Ana saca muchas fotos con su
   _____ .

3. A Javier le gusta la cámara de Ana porque no
   es muy _____ .

4. Ana y Javier van a un _____ para
   escribirle a Esteban por _____ electrónico.

5. Según Ana, el ordenador _____
   para mucho.

6. Javier quiere saber qué tal fue el _____
   de Cristina.

© Pearson Education, Inc. All rights reserved.

Realidades B

Capítulo 9B

Nombre

Fecha

Hora

VIDEO

Y, ¿qué más?

Actividad 4

You heard Ana and Javier talk about the many ways they use computers. Write a paragraph describing your two favorite ways to use a computer. Use the model to give you an idea of how to start.

Modelo   *En mi casa todos usan la computadora. Para mí el uso más importante es...*

_____

_____

_____

_____

_____

_____

© Pearson Education, Inc. All rights reserved.

Nombre _____ Hora _____

Fecha _____

AUDIO

Actividad 5

While navigating a new Web site, two friends click on a link to a self-quiz to find out if they are **CiberAdictos.** Based on their discussion of each question, write in the chart below whether you think they answered **sí** or **no**. According to the Web site, a score of more than six **sí** answers determines that you are a **CiberAdicto.** You will hear each set of statements twice.

	1	2	3	4	5	6	7	8	¿Es CiberAdicto?
Rafael									
Miguel									

Actividad 6

Víctor has studied for the first quiz in his beginning technology class. As the teacher reads each statement, he is to answer **falso** or **cierto**. Listen to the statements and write the answers in the boxes, and take the quiz too. Would you be able to score 100%? You will hear each statement twice.

1	2	3	4	5	6	7	8	9	10

Actividad 7

Listen to the following conversations that you overhear while sitting at a table in the Café Mariposa. After listening to what each person is saying, write what they asked for in the first column and what they were served in the second column. You will hear each statement twice.

Persona	Comida pedida	Comida servida
1. Señor Cruz		
2. Señora Vargas		
3. Señor Ávila		
4. Marcelo y Daniele		
5. Señor Urbina		
6. Señora Campos		
7. Señora Suerte		

© Pearson Education, Inc. All rights reserved.

Nombre _____ Hora _____

Fecha _____

Actividad 8

Listen as teenagers talk to each other about what they need to learn how to do. The second teenager is always able to suggest someone whom the first teenager should ask for help. Match the person who is suggested to the correct picture. You will hear each set of statements twice.

_____ _____ _____

_____ _____ _____

Actividad 9

Listen as two people discuss how the computer and the Internet have changed our lives. As you listen, organize their points into two columns by summarizing what they say. You will hear each set of statements twice.

Antes de la computadora y la Red	Después de la computadora y la Red
1. _____	_____
2. _____	_____
3. _____	_____
4. _____	_____

© Pearson Education, Inc. All rights reserved.

Realidades B

Capítulo 9B

Nombre _____

Hora _____

Fecha _____

WRITING

Actividad 10

Read the following ad about a computer of the future. Then, answer the questions below.

CEREBRADOR: ¡EL FUTURO AHORA!

¿Está cansado de ver las computadoras del futuro en una película o de leer sobre ellas en una novela? ¿Quiere el futuro ahora? ¡Pues **Cerebrador** lo tiene!

♦ La información, los gráficos, la música en la Red...
   ¡todo sin límite!

♦ Grabar un disco, escribir un informe, navegar en la Red...
   ¡sólo hay que pensarlo y se logra en poco tiempo!

♦ ¿Tiene problemas de conexión o detesta sentarse a usar la computadora?
   Sólo necesita **Cerebrador** *y dos metros de espacio para poder ver todo en la pantalla: documentos, correo electrónico, su página Web, etc. Conecte a su propia cabeza.*

Con **Cerebrador** puede sacar fotos con una minicámara digital y crear diapositivas con ellas.

Llame ahora para pedir este fenómeno.

---

1. ¿Cómo se llama la computadora del anuncio?

_____

2. ¿Qué dice el anuncio que Ud. puede hacer con esta computadora?

_____

_____

3. ¿Qué necesita para usar una computadora? ¿Es una computadora portátil?

_____

_____

_____

4. ¿Cree Ud. que es posible comprar una computadora como ésta? ¿Por qué?

_____

_____

_____

© Pearson Education, Inc. All rights reserved.

Communication Workbook

© Pearson Education, Inc. All rights reserved.

WRITING

Actividad 11

Your favorite restaurant has great food, but the wait staff is always messing up the orders. Using the pictures as clues and the correct forms of the verbs **pedir** and **servir**, write what happens when the following people order their meals. Follow the model and remember to use the proper indirect object pronouns in your sentences.

Yo   El camarero

Modelo
Yo pido pescado pero el camarero me sirve pollo.

1.   Tú   Ellos

2.   Nosotros   La camarera

3.   María   Uds.

4.   Ellos   Nosotros

5.   Ramón y Yo   Los camareros

Nombre _____   Hora _____

Fecha _____   **WRITING**

Actividad 12

Answer the following questions in 2–3 complete sentences using the verbs **saber** and/or **conocer**.

1. ¿Eres talentoso(a)? ¿Qué sabes hacer? ¿Tienes unos amigos muy talentosos? ¿Qué saben hacer ellos?

_____

_____

_____

_____

2. ¿Conoces a alguna persona famosa? ¿Quién? ¿Cómo es? ¿Alguien más en tu familia conoce a una persona famosa?

_____

_____

_____

_____

3. ¿Qué ciudades o países conocen tú y tu familia? ¿Cuándo los visitaste? ¿Qué lugares conocen tus amigos?

_____

_____

_____

_____

4. ¿Qué sabes de la geografía de Latinoamérica? (¿Sabes cuál es la capital de Uruguay? ¿Sabes cuántos países hay en Sudamérica?)

_____

_____

_____

_____

© Pearson Education, Inc. All rights reserved.

Realidades B

Capítulo 9B

Nombre _____

Fecha _____

Hora _____

WRITING

Actividad 13

Describe the **cibercafé** below. First, tell three things that you can do there. Next, tell three items that they serve at the café, using the verb **servir** and the food items in the picture. Finally, tell what you can do if you need assistance at the **cibercafé.** Use the verb **pedir**, and the verbs **saber** and **conocer** to discuss how knowledgeable the staff is (**Ellos saben ayudar.../ Ellos conocen bien la Red...**).

Ud. puede _____

_____

_____

_____

Allí ellos _____

_____

_____

_____

_____

_____

_____

_____

© Pearson Education, Inc. All rights reserved.

Notes

Notes

Notes

Notes

Notes

Notes

Notes

Notes

Notes

Notes

Notes

Notes

Notes

Notes

Notes

Notes

Notes

Test Preparation

Table of Contents

Tema 5: Fiesta en familia

Capítulo 5A: Una fiesta de cumpleaños

Reading Skills 131

Integrated Performance Assessment 133

Practice Test 134

Capítulo 5B: ¡Vamos a un restaurante!

Reading Skills 138

Integrated Performance Assessment 140

Practice Test 141

Tema 6: La casa

Capítulo 6A: En mi dormitorio

Reading Skills 144

Integrated Performance Assessment 146

Practice Test 147

Capítulo 6B: ¿Cómo es tu casa?

Reading Skills 150

Integrated Performance Assessment 152

Practice Test 153

Tema 7: De compras

Capítulo 7A: ¿Cuánto cuesta?

Reading Skills 156

Integrated Performance Assessment 158

Practice Test 159

Capítulo 7B: ¡Qué regalo!

Reading Skills 162

Integrated Performance Assessment 164

Practice Test 165

© Pearson Education, Inc. All rights reserved.

Tema 8: Experiencias

Capítulo 8A: De vacaciones

Reading Skills 168

Integrated Performance Assessment 170

Practice Test 171

Capítulo 8B: Ayudando en la comunidad

Reading Skills 175

Integrated Performance Assessment 177

Practice Test 178

Tema 9: Medios de comunicación

Capítulo 9A: El cine y la televisión

Reading Skills 181

Integrated Performance Assessment 183

Practice Test 184

Capítulo 9B: La tecnología

Reading Skills 187

Integrated Performance Assessment 189

Practice Test 190

© Pearson Education, Inc. All rights reserved.

To the Student

Did you know that becoming a better reader in Spanish can improve your scores on standardized reading tests in English? Research has shown that the skills you develop by reading in a second language are transferred to reading in your first language. Research also shows that the more you practice for standardized tests and work on test-taking strategies, the more your scores will improve. The goal of this book is to help you improve your test-taking strategies and to provide extra practice with readings in both Spanish and English.

Getting to Know the Test

The practice tests in this book offer a variety of readings to reflect the types of passages you might expect to find on a standardized test. They also provide practice for three different types of questions you are apt to encounter on such a test: multiple choice, Short Response, and Extended Response.

Multiple Choice Multiple choice questions always have four answer choices. Pick the one that is the best answer. A correct answer is worth 1 point.

Short Response This symbol appears next to questions requiring short written answers:

This symbol appears next to questions requiring short written answers that are a creative extension based on the reading:

Take approximately 3 to 5 minutes to answer a Short Response question. Read all parts of the question carefully, plan your answer, then write the answer in your own words. A complete answer to a Short Response question is worth 2 points. A partial answer is worth 1 or 0 points.

© Pearson Education, Inc. All rights reserved.

NOTE: <u>If a Short Response question is written in English, write your answer in English, unless the instructions tell you to do otherwise. If it is written in Spanish, write your answer in Spanish.</u>

Extended Response This symbol appears next to questions requiring longer written answers based on information that can be inferred from the reading:

This symbol appears next to questions requiring longer written answers that are a creative extension based on the reading:

Take approximately 5 to 15 minutes to answer an Extended Response question. A complete answer is worth 4 points. A partial answer is worth 3, 2, 1, or 0 points.

NOTE: <u>If an Extended Response question is written in English, write your answer in English. If it is written in Spanish, write your answer in Spanish.</u>

Taking These Practice Tests

Your teacher will assign a test for classwork or homework, or you might be taking these tests on your own. Each reading is followed by questions, and the Practice Test Answer Sheet immediately follows the questions. For multiple choice questions, you should bubble-in the response. For Short and Extended Response questions, write your answers on the lines provided.

Tips for Improving Your Score

Know the Rules

Learn the rules for any test you take. For example, depending on how a test is scored, it may or may not be advisable to guess if you are not sure of the correct answer. Find that out before you begin the exam. Be sure you understand:

- how much time is allowed for the test
- the types of questions that will be asked
- how the questions should be answered
- how they will be scored

© Pearson Education, Inc. All rights reserved.

Know Yourself and Make a Plan

Ask yourself: "How will I prepare for the test?" First, ask your teacher to help you list your strengths and weaknesses on tests. Then make a detailed plan for practicing or reviewing. Give yourself plenty of time to prepare. Don't leave everything until the night before. Set aside blocks of uninterrupted time for studying, with short breaks at regular intervals.

Before the Test

Do something relaxing the night before. Then get a good night's sleep, and be sure to eat a nutritious meal before the test. Wear comfortable clothing. If possible, wear a watch or sit where you can see a clock. Make sure you have all the materials you will need. Find out in advance if you will need a certain type of pencil, for example, and bring several with you—already sharpened. Be sure you know where the test is being given and at what time. Plan to arrive early.

Know What You Are Being Asked

There are two basic types of test questions: objective, one-right-answer questions and essay questions. It is essential that you read <u>all</u> questions carefully. Ask yourself, "What are they asking me?" The purpose of a standardized reading test is to determine:

- how well you understand what you read
- how well you are able to use the critical thinking and problem-solving skills that are so critical for success in today's world

Here is a list of basic reading skills:

- Understanding major ideas, details, and organization
- Drawing conclusions
- Understanding cause and effect
- Comparing and contrasting
- Finding, interpreting, and organizing information
- Understanding author's purpose and/or viewpoint
- Understanding character and plot development

Always read the questions <u>before</u> you read the passage. This will help you focus on the task. If it is allowed, ask your teacher to explain any directions you do not understand.

Watch Your Time

Allot a specific amount of time per question—approximately 1 minute for multiple choice, 3 to 5 minutes for Short Response, and 5 to 15 minutes for Extended Response. Do not spend too much time on any one question, and monitor your time so that you will be able to complete the test.

© Pearson Education, Inc. All rights reserved.

Show What You Know, Relax, and Think Positively

Answer those questions that you are sure about first. If a question seems too difficult, skip it and return to it later. Remember that while some questions may seem hard, others will be easy. You may never learn to love taking tests, but you can control the situation and make sure that you reach your full potential for success.

Above all, relax. It's natural to be nervous, but think positively. Just do your best.

Multiple Choice Questions: Helpful Hints

Multiple choice questions have only one right answer. There is no "creative" response, only a correct one. This book provides extensive practice for the types of multiple choice items that you might find on a standardized reading test. There are four answer choices (A, B, C, D or F, G, H, J) per question. Allot approximately 1 minute to answer a multiple choice question. Answers are worth 1 point each.

- Read the question carefully.
- Try to identify the answer <u>before</u> you examine the choices.
- Eliminate obviously incorrect choices by lightly crossing them out.
- Try to narrow the choices down to two.
- Depending on how a test is to be scored, you may or may not want to guess (for these practice tests, check that you will **not** be penalized for guessing wrong).

Short and Extended Response: Helpful Hints

The dreaded essay question will probably not be as difficult as expected if you follow these strategies:

- Read the question <u>before</u> reading the passage.
- Re-read the question as you prepare to respond: Are you being asked to list, describe, explain, discuss, persuade, or compare and contrast? These are very different things.
- Look back at the passage as often as necessary to answer the question correctly. Underline any key sections that you think might be important to your response.
- Use the margins next to the passage to jot down thoughts and ideas and to prepare a brief outline of what you will include in your answer. Use a clear, direct introduction that answers the specific question being asked. As a start, try turning the question into a statement. Include both general ideas and specific details from the reading in your answer.

© Pearson Education, Inc. All rights reserved.

- Review your response to make sure you have expressed your thoughts well. Is your introduction clear? Have you stated the general idea(s)? Have you included supporting details?
- If your response is in Spanish, check for grammar errors (subject-verb agreement, adjective agreement, correct verb endings and tenses). In either language, proofread your answer for correct spelling.

How the Test Will Be Scored

It is important to know in advance how responses will be scored. This will lower your anxiety level and help you focus. For the purpose of these practice tests, you can assume the following:

Multiple Choice Questions
Multiple choice answers are either right or wrong. You will receive credit and 1 point if you select the correct answer.

Performance-Based Questions (Short and Extended Response)
Short and Extended Response questions are called "performance tasks." They are often scored with rubrics, which describe a range of performance. You will receive credit for how close your answers come to the desired response. The performance tasks on these practice tests will require thoughtful answers. You must:
- <u>Read</u> the passage
- <u>Think</u> about the question as it relates to the passage, and
- <u>Explain</u> your answer by citing general ideas and specific details from the passage

or:
- <u>Create</u> a written document (a letter, for example) that clearly uses or models information provided in the reading passage

Rubric for Short Response Questions

2 points The response indicates that the student has a complete understanding of the reading concept embodied in the task. The student has provided a response that is accurate, complete, and fulfills all the requirements of the task. Necessary support and/or examples are included, and the information given is clearly text-based. Any extensions beyond the text are relevant to the task.

© Pearson Education, Inc. All rights reserved.

1 point   The response indicates that the student has a partial understanding of the reading concept embodied in the task. The student has provided a response that may include information that is essentially correct and text-based, but the information is too general or too simplistic. Some of the support and/or examples may be incomplete or omitted.

0 points   The response is inaccurate, confused, and/or irrelevant, or the student has failed to respond to the task.

Rubric for Extended Response Questions

4 points   The response indicates that the student has a thorough understanding of the reading concept embodied in the task. The student has provided a response that is accurate, complete, and fulfills all the requirements of the task. Necessary support and/or examples are included, and the information given is clearly text-based. Any extensions beyond the text are relevant to the task.

3 points   The response indicates that the student has an understanding of the reading concept embodied in the task. The student has provided a response that is accurate and fulfills all the requirements of the task, but the required support and/or details are not complete or clearly text-based.

2 points   The response indicates that the student has a partial understanding of the reading concept embodied in the task. The student has provided a response that may include information that is essentially correct and text-based, but the information is too general or too simplistic. Some of the support and/or examples and requirements of the task may be incomplete or omitted.

1 point   The response indicates that the student has very limited understanding of the reading concept embodied in the task. The response is incomplete, may exhibit many flaws, and may not address all requirements of the task.

0 points   The response is inaccurate, confused, and/or irrelevant, or the student has failed to respond to the task.

© Pearson Education, Inc. All rights reserved.

Getting Started

So let's get started. If there was anything in this Introduction that you did not understand, ask your teacher about it. Glance once again at the Helpful Hints before taking the first test. In fact, it will be helpful if you review those hints each time you take one of these tests. And remember: The more you practice, the higher your scores will be.

¡Buena suerte!

© Pearson Education, Inc. All rights reserved.

Realidades **B**   Nombre _____   Fecha _____

Capítulo 5A   **Reading Skills:**
Exploración del lenguaje, p. 52

Strategies to Analyze Words: Context and Word Structure Clues

It is impossible to know the meaning of every word in a language. Good readers develop strategies to determine the meanings of unknown words in their reading without having to look them up in the dictionary. Good readers also know that their guesses may be wrong, so they develop strategies to check their guesses. Then, they use more traditional methods of finding the word's meaning: looking it up in the dictionary or asking for assistance from someone trustworthy.

Tip

Knowing the English equivalent of common Spanish suffixes can help you build your vocabulary both in English and Spanish. For example, page 52 of your textbook features the section **Exploración del lenguaje,** about Spanish diminutives. The suffix *-ito* or *-ita* in a Spanish word can be used to show affection for that particular person or thing, or it can be used to indicate that the person or thing is little or small in size. Likewise, in English, the suffix *-ette* can indicate that a person or thing is little or small in size; the suffixes *-y* or *-ie* can be used to show affection for a person or thing.

You must be aware that just because an English word ends with *-ette*, *-y*, or *-ie*, does not mean that the suffixes can always translate to a term of affection or to something small. When making an educated guess about an unusual word, you should always test your guess in context. In other words, you should insert your guessed meaning into the actual sentence where you found the unusual word.

1. Read the following sentence: When I am with my <u>sweetie</u>, the days always seem <u>rosy</u>. Only one of the underlined words uses the *-ie* or *-y* suffix as a term of affection. Which one is it? Now read this sentence: "The artist hardly needed any paint from his <u>palette</u> to paint the <u>statuette</u>." Only one of the underlined words uses the *-ette* suffix to indicate something small in size. Which one is it?

Sample question:

2. Read the passage below and answer the question that follows.

Fred's mom is blond, and his aunt is <u>brunette</u>. Fred loves his aunt, and she is crazy about him. "Come visit me, <u>Freddy</u>!" she'll often say over the telephone. Whenever Fred visits her in her small apartment, she always has a special <u>chocolatey</u> treat waiting for him in her <u>kitchenette</u>.

Based on your understanding of the underlined words in the passage, which statement below is TRUE?
A Fred's aunt is short with brown hair.
B Freddy is small in size.
C "Chocolatey" is a term of affection.
D The aunt's kitchen is small in size.

© Pearson Education, Inc. All rights reserved.

Determining the Main Idea and Identifying Relevant Details

To know the relevant details in a reading passage is to know which ones are most important. The first step in identifying the relevant details is to identify the main idea of the passage. The relevant details are the ones that help support the main idea. After reading a passage, good readers ask themselves, "What is this passage mostly about?" and "Which details in the passage help support, explain, or prove the main idea?"

Tip

Some readers are better able to identify the main idea and the relevant details when they have a graphic organizer. The graphic organizer below is a cluster or a web where the main idea is the central circle and the relevant details sprout out from the center like spokes on a wheel.

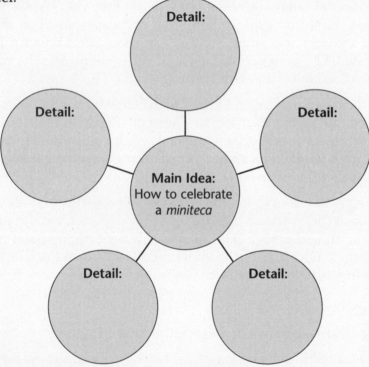

1. On pages 54–55 in your textbook, re-read the **Lectura**, *¡Te invitamos a nuestra miniteca!* The main idea of this passage is about how to celebrate a special occasion with a *miniteca*. Use the cluster graphic organizer above to list any relevant details in the passage that show the features of a *miniteca* celebration.

Sample question:

2. Which is NOT one of the relevant details featured in the **Lectura** about celebrating a special occasion with a *miniteca*?
   A Guests pay a small fee to attend.
   B It can be celebrated at a house or at a special location.
   C Lights, decorations, and music help create a festive atmosphere.
   D Parents spend time with the young people.

© Pearson Education, Inc. All rights reserved.

Integrated Performance Assessment
Unit theme: Una fiesta de cumpleaños

Context for the Integrated Performance Assessment: An exchange student from Mexico is spending a semester at your school. The Spanish Club is in charge of planning several special activities for her. Her birthday is next month and you are on the committee in charge of planning the celebration.

Interpretive Task: Watch the *Videohistoria: ¡Feliz cumpleaños!* from *Realidades 1, DVD 3, Capítulo 5A* (without the words displayed) to see how Cristina celebrates her birthday. Make a list of what the club needs to plan the party as well as the activities that are going to take place during the party. You should have at least 8 items on your list.

Interpersonal Task: Discuss your list with the 2 or 3 other members of the committee. Listen to the committee's suggestions and add a few new ideas to your list.

Presentational Task: Make an oral presentation to the members of the Spanish Club describing what the members need to get for the party and what they are going to do during the party.

Interpersonal Task Rubric

	Score: 1 Does not meet expectations	Score: 3 Meets expectations	Score: 5 Exceeds expectations
Language Use	Student uses little or no target language and relies heavily on native language word order.	Student uses the target language consistently, but may mix native and target language word order.	Student uses the target language exclusively and integrates target language word order into conversation.
Vocabulary Use	Student uses limited and repetitive language.	Student uses only recently acquired vocabulary.	Student uses both recently and previously acquired vocabulary.

Presentational Task Rubric

	Score: 1 Does not meet expectations	Score: 3 Meets expectations	Score: 5 Exceeds expectations
Amount of Communication	Student gives limited or no details about what students will need for the party and what they will do at the party.	Student gives adequate details about what students will need for the party and what they will do at the party.	Student gives consistent details about what students will need for the party and what they will do at the party.
Accuracy	Student's accuracy with vocabulary and structures is limited.	Student's accuracy with vocabulary and structures is adequate.	Student's accuracy with vocabulary and structures is exemplary.
Comprehensibility	Student's ideas lack clarity and are difficult to understand.	Student's ideas are adequately clear and fairly well understood.	Student's ideas are precise and easily understood.
Vocabulary Use	Student uses limited and repetitive vocabulary.	Student uses only recently acquired vocabulary.	Student uses both recently and previously acquired vocabulary.

© Pearson Education, Inc. All rights reserved.

Capítulo 5A   **Practice Test**

Holidays in the Hispanic World

1   Some holidays are celebrated differently in Latin America and Spain than in the United States. *La Nochebuena,* or Christmas Eve, for example, is when most of the Spanish-speaking world celebrates Christmas. A nativity scene (*un nacimiento* or *un pesebre*) is a common decoration in homes. It may be small—the Dominican Republic is known for its truly miniature figures—or large enough to fill an entire room or patio. But large or small, it is often very elaborate, with hills, trees, roads, little houses, and small mirrors to represent ponds. *El nacimiento* is usually the focal point of the festivities, with family gathered around to sing carols to the accompaniment of a guitar or a bamboo pipe or maracas. Colored paper lanterns, balloons, piñatas, and dancing are often part of the evening celebration.

2   Epiphany (*el Día de los Reyes*), on January 6, marks the formal end of the Christmas holidays. Traditionally, it was the day on which children in Spanish-speaking countries received their gifts, because it commemorates the arrival of the Three Kings into Bethlehem with their gifts of gold, frankincense, and myrrh. Today, however, in more and more homes, gifts are opened on Christmas Day or on Christmas Eve.

3   In much of Latin America, the weather is warm during the end-of-year holidays (below the equator it is the beginning of summer) and *el Año Nuevo* may be celebrated with fireworks and even barbecues. In Spain, it is the custom to eat twelve grapes at the stroke of midnight, one grape each time the clock chimes.

4   *El Día de la Raza,* October 12, celebrates the blending of the Spanish and indigenous cultures that resulted from Columbus's landing

in the Americas. It is sometimes called *el Día de la Hispanidad*. In recent years, however, it has become of less importance than specific national holidays. *El Día de la Independencia* is, of course, celebrated on different days in different countries. For example, September 15 is the national holiday of four Central American nations: Guatemala, Honduras, El Salvador, and Nicaragua. Paraguay celebrates its independence from Spain on May 14; Argentina, May 25; Venezuela, July 5; Colombia, July 20; Peru, July 28; Bolivia, August 6; Ecuador, August 10; Mexico, September 16; and Chile and Costa Rica, September 18. The Dominican Republic celebrates its independence from Haiti on February 27; Uruguay, its independence from Brazil on August 25; Panama, its independence from Colombia on November 3. And Spain's national holiday? *El Día de la Hispanidad*—October 12.

5   Another major fall holiday is *el Día de los Muertos* (All Souls' Day) on November 2. This holiday is a day of remembrance for all those who have died. It is a very special celebration in Mexico. There are, of course, prayers, religious services, and visits to the cemetery. Families build special altars, called *ofrendas,* in their homes. These *ofrendas* are decorated with flowers and candles, but they are not at all solemn. Photographs of loved ones who have died are displayed among objects that they cherished or used most—a rocking chair, for example, or reading glasses, gardening tools, or cooking utensils. *El Día de los Muertos* is also celebrated by eating a sweetened bread—*el pan de muerto*—which is either shaped like skulls and crosses, or decorated with white sugar candies in the shape of skulls, crosses, coffins, and tombs. For children, there are white masks, tin or

© Pearson Education, Inc. All rights reserved.

Holidays in the Hispanic World (*continued*)

wire skeletons attached to strings, and even toy coffins that contain a skeleton that jumps out when a string is pulled.

6   In the calendar of the Catholic Church, almost every day is dedicated to one or more saints. A person's "saint's day," or *santo*, is the day dedicated to the saint who has that person's name (or one derived from it). For example, *el santo* for every José, Josefina, or Josefa is St. Joseph's Day (March 19), and *el santo* for every Pablo, Paulo, Paulina, and Paula is St. Paul's Day (June 29). Traditionally, part of a person's name was determined by the saint's day on which he or she was born. For example, if a girl whose family planned to name her María Luisa happened to be born on May 30—St. Ferdinand's Day—she would likely be named María Luisa Fernanda to honor that saint. In fact, the traditional Mexican "Happy Birthday" song, *Las mañanitas*, is actually a song for a saint's day.

7   This custom is disappearing, however, and a person's birthday and saint's day are often not the same. In many countries, a person's saint's day is considered more important than a birthday. Even non-Catholics may celebrate their *santo*, for no one wants to miss out on his or her special day for a party and a few gifts. So truly every day is *un día de fiesta en el mundo hispano!*

© Pearson Education, Inc. All rights reserved.

Capítulo 5A   **Practice Test**

Answer questions 1–6. Base your answers on the reading *"Holidays in the Hispanic World."*

1 In a traditional Latin American home, which of the following most closely compares with the Christmas tree in a traditional U.S. home?

    A   *la Nochebuena*

    B   *el nacimiento*

    C   *la piñata*

    D   *el Día de los Reyes*

2 Which one of the following statements is true?

    F   All of the nations of Central America have the same Independence Day.

    G   In the United States, the best-known national holiday among the Latin American nations is *el Día de los Reyes.*

    H   Of the nations of Latin America, all but two celebrate their national holiday within the five-month period from May to September.

    J   All of the Spanish-speaking countries of Latin America got their independence from Spain.

3 What holiday in the United States has the same underlying purpose as *el Día de los Muertos?*

    A   the Fourth of July

    B   Memorial Day

    C   Labor Day

    D   Veterans' Day

4 Complete this statement: Today a person's *santo* is most often

    F   a saint's birthday.

    G   his or her own birthday.

    H   the day dedicated to the saint who has the same or a similar name.

    J   either March 19, May 30, or June 29.

5 **READ THINK EXPLAIN** October 12 was once a fairly major holiday throughout the Americas. Why do you suppose that in most countries the national holiday has become of greater importance than Columbus Day? Do you think this is a good thing or a bad thing? Why?

6 **READ THINK EXPLAIN** If you live far to the north or to the south of the equator, there are considerable differences in the way in which you might celebrate the end-of-year holidays. Explain why and describe at least three of those differences.

© Pearson Education, Inc. All rights reserved.

Capítulo 5A   **Practice Test Answer Sheet**

1 Ⓐ Ⓑ Ⓒ Ⓓ   **2** Ⓕ Ⓖ Ⓗ Ⓙ   **3** Ⓐ Ⓑ Ⓒ Ⓓ

4 Ⓕ Ⓖ Ⓗ Ⓙ

5

READ
THINK
EXPLAIN

_____
_____
_____
_____
_____
_____

6

READ
THINK
EXPLAIN

_____
_____
_____
_____
_____
_____
_____
_____
_____

© Pearson Education, Inc. All rights reserved.

Identifying Methods of Development and Patterns of Organization

Good readers understand the tools and techniques of authors. To identify the methods of development used by an author in a text, good readers must first determine the author's purpose by asking, "Why was this text written?" After determining the author's purpose, readers next ask, "What techniques did the author use to achieve his or her purpose?" These techniques are known as methods of development and could include, among other things, the organization pattern, the word choice, or the sentence structure used in the text.

Tip

One common pattern of organization for writers is the process paper. The process paper could be a set of instructions, a recipe, a "how-to" guide, or even the summary of a story. In a process paper, you explain the steps in a process. A graphic organizer known as a flow chart helps you keep track of all those steps. The flow chart also helps you see which steps come first in the process and which ones follow.

1. After re-reading the recipe for *Arroz con leche* in **Actividad 25 "*Un postre delicioso*"** on page 81 in your textbook, fill in the recipe steps in the flow chart below.

Six steps for making *Arroz con leche*

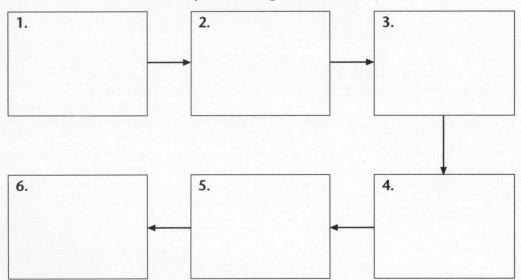

Sample question:

2. According to the recipe for *Arroz con leche*, when should the cook add the sugar and vanilla to the rice?

   A Before cooking it slowly for one hour.

   B After putting it in the refrigerator.

   C After cooking it slowly for one hour.

   D While soaking the rice for one hour and a half.

© Pearson Education, Inc. All rights reserved.

Making and Confirming Inferences

One indication of good readers is their ability to read between the lines of a text. Not only do they literally read and comprehend what a text says, but they also make inferences from what they read. An inference is an educated guess about something written in the text. An inference, because it is a guess, can never be absolutely right or wrong. However, an inference, like a conclusion, can be believable based upon the evidence that is present in the text. Confirming an inference means locating the evidence in the text that lends support to the inference.

Tip

One strategy that helps students as they make and confirm inferences is a two-column note activity known as Opinion-Proof. As you read, you formulate educated guesses or opinions about what you have read. Jot these down on the Opinion side of your notes. If your opinions are believable, then you should be able to write down on the Proof side all the evidence you find in the reading passage that lends support to your opinion or inference.

1. On page 84 in your textbook, read the **Lectura, *Una visita a Santa Fe.*** Based on what you have read, fill in the missing blanks of the Opinion-Proof chart below.

Opinion	Proof
Alicia and Pedro are good cousins to Rosario and Luis.	_____
	_____
_____	*¡No sabemos bailar pero va a ser muy divertido!*
_____	
_____	*¡Los cinco días van a pasar rápidamente!*

Sample question:

2. Based on the information presented in the letter from Alicia and Pedro to Rosario and Luis, the reader can infer that

   A Santa Fe is a city with over 400 years of history and culture.

   B Rosario and Luis will likely be bored during their visit to Santa Fe.

   C Alicia and Pedro are not easily embarrassed.

   D the *fandango* is a dance better known for its excitement than for its history.

© Pearson Education, Inc. All rights reserved.

Integrated Performance Assessment
Unit theme: ¡Vamos a un restaurante!

Context for the Integrated Performance Assessment: Angélica is a Spanish-speaking student from San Antonio, Texas. She and her family love to go to their favorite restaurant, Casa Río. She wants to know if your favorite restaurant is similar to her favorite restaurant.

Interpretive Task: Watch the *Videohistoria: En el Restaurante Casa Río* (without the words displayed) from *Realidades 1, DVD 3, Capítulo 5B*. You will see Angélica and her family dining at Casa Río. Look carefully for similarities and differences between Casa Río and your favorite restaurant. Make a list of the similarities and differences you see and hear.

Interpersonal Task: Tell your partner the name of your favorite restaurant. Describe the similarities and differences between Casa Río and your favorite restaurant. Listen to your partner's description. Ask each other questions in order to find more similarities and differences.

Presentational Task: Write an e-mail to Angélica telling her about your favorite restaurant and how it is similar to and different from Casa Río.

Interpersonal Task Rubric

	Score: 1 Does not meet expectations	Score: 3 Meets expectations	Score: 5 Exceeds expectations
Language Use	Student uses little or no target language and relies heavily on native language word order.	Student uses the target language consistently, but may mix native and target language word order.	Student uses the target language exclusively and integrates target language word order into conversation.
Vocabulary Use	Student uses limited and repetitive language.	Student uses only recently acquired vocabulary.	Student uses both recently and previously acquired vocabulary.

Presentational Task Rubric

	Score: 1 Does not meet expectations	Score: 3 Meets expectations	Score: 5 Exceeds expectations
Amount of Communication	Student gives limited or no details about how different or similar his/her favorite restaurant is to Casa Río.	Student gives adequate details about how different or similar his/her favorite restaurant is to Casa Río.	Student gives consistent details about how different or similar his/her favorite restaurant is to Casa Río.
Accuracy	Student's accuracy with vocabulary and structures is limited.	Student's accuracy with vocabulary and structures is adequate.	Student's accuracy with vocabulary and structures is exemplary.
Comprehensibility	Student's ideas lack clarity and are difficult to understand.	Student's ideas are adequately clear and fairly well understood.	Student's ideas are precise and easily understood.
Vocabulary Use	Student uses limited and repetitive vocabulary.	Student uses only recently acquired vocabulary.	Student uses both recently and previously acquired vocabulary.

© Pearson Education, Inc. All rights reserved.

Communication Workbook

EL SOL, viernes 18 de julio

NOTICIAS DE CELEBRACIONES

Esta semana en San Antonio muchas familias celebran ocasiones muy especiales.

Quinceañera

Mirella Lugo Armas, hija de Humberto Lugo Díaz y Carmen Armas Garza de Lugo, celebra sus quince años el domingo 20 de julio a las 6:00 P.M. en el restaurante Casa Estrella. Hay una gran fiesta con una banda de música tejana después de la cena.

Boda

Dolores Lara Villarreal y Roberto Pastor Peña celebran su boda en la iglesia de San Antonio, el sábado 19 de julio a las 8:00 P.M. Después de la ceremonia hay una fiesta con música y una cena en casa de la familia Lara.

Día del santo

Santiago Paredes Sánchez celebra el día de su santo el viernes 25 de julio. Hay una comida en su honor en casa de sus abuelos a las 2:00 P.M.

Graduación

Ana Luisa Martínez Puente celebra su graduación de la Memorial High School el día 22 de julio. Después de la graduación hay una barbacoa para la familia y los amigos en el parque Fiesta Texas a las 4:00 P.M.

Cincuenta años

Roberto González Juárez y María Luisa Gallardo Correa de González celebran su aniversario de bodas el 25 de julio en el salón de fiestas La Suerte. Van a celebrar la ocasión con una comida deliciosa para la familia y los amigos.

© Pearson Education, Inc. All rights reserved.

Realidades **B**

Capítulo 5B **Practice Test**

Answer questions 1–6. Base your answers on the reading *"Noticias de celebraciones."*

1 Which of the celebrations has a party outside?

    A *cincuenta años*

    B *graduación*

    C *día del santo*

    D *quinceañera*

2 What do all of the notices of celebrations have in common?

    F They all mention a meal.

    G They all mention music.

    H They all take place in the evening.

    J They all mention a ceremony.

3 Which of these occasions is celebrated only in the Hispanic culture?

    A *boda*

    B *cincuenta años*

    C *quinceañera*

    D *graduación*

4 Which of the celebrations mentions the names of the parents of the honored person or people?

    F *graduación*

    G *quinceañera*

    H *día del santo*

    J *boda*

5 READ THINK EXPLAIN   Which of these celebrations do you think might have more guests that are family members than friends? Why do you think these celebrations might be more for family members?

6 READ THINK EXPLAIN   Clasifica las fiestas de 5 a 1. El 5 es para la fiesta más formal, y el 1 es para la fiesta menos formal. Explica tus clasificaciones "5" y "1".

            Communication Workbook

© Pearson Education, Inc. All rights reserved.

1 Ⓐ Ⓑ Ⓒ Ⓓ   **2** Ⓕ Ⓖ Ⓗ Ⓙ   **3** Ⓐ Ⓑ Ⓒ Ⓓ

4 Ⓕ Ⓖ Ⓗ Ⓙ

5

READ
THINK
EXPLAIN

_____

_____

_____

_____

_____

_____

6

READ
THINK
EXPLAIN

_____

_____

_____

_____

_____

_____

_____

_____

_____

© Pearson Education, Inc. All rights reserved.

Locates, Gathers, Analyzes, and Evaluates Written Information

By showing that they can locate, gather, analyze, and evaluate information from one or more reading passages, good readers demonstrate that they know how to conduct research. On a test, readers are often asked to locate, gather, analyze, and evaluate information from a reading passage and then show how to put that information to good use.

Tip

Readers who conduct research are skilled at translating information from their reading into their own words. If they encounter information in one format, such as a chart, they are able to restate that information in a different format, such as in sentences or as bullets. This is how they demonstrate their comprehension of what they have read.

1. Review **Actividad 33** "*¿Duermes bien?*" on page 114, and then complete the two exercises below.

   Use four sentences to restate some of the information presented in the two pie graphs.

   _____

   _____

   _____

   _____

   Use one paragraph with a topic sentence and supporting sentences to restate the information presented as bullets.

   _____

   _____

   _____

   _____

   _____

   _____

   _____

Sample question:

2. Imagine that a friend was sleeping only 5–6 hours on school nights. Which information from the graphs and bullets in **Actividad 33** would be LEAST likely to make your friend start sleeping more?

   A Las personas que duermen menos de seis horas por noche sufren más lesiones.

   B 52% de las personas duermen ocho horas o más en los fines de la semana.

   C Las personas que duermen menos de seis horas por noche tienen más problemas de relaciones interpersonales.

   D Solamente 15% de las personas duermen menos de seis horas durante la semana.

© Pearson Education, Inc. All rights reserved.

Understanding Tone

To understand an author's tone in a reading passage, good readers focus not just on what is said, but also on how it is said. Like identifying an author's point of view, identifying an author's tone requires readers to ask, "What is the author's attitude or feelings about the subject of the reading passage?" First, readers should be able to identify when an author feels positive, negative, or neutral toward a subject. As readers gain more practice with this skill, they should be able to identify a wide range of tones used by authors. Some of these might include: admiration, nostalgia, objectivity, sarcasm, surprise, and sympathy.

Tip

One way to begin to understand an author's tone is to separate the statements of fact from the statements of opinion. While statements of fact make an author seem more objective, statements of opinion often express the author's feelings about a subject.

1. After reviewing the **Lectura,** *El desastre en mi dormitorio* on pages 116–117 in your textbook, identify the statements from the reading passage as facts or opinions. Then, for each opinion, identify the feelings that it reveals about the author.

	Fact or Opinion	Feelings Expressed by Opinions
Rosario: *"Estoy desesperada."*	_____	_____
Rosario: *"Hay pizza debajo de la cama."*	_____	_____
Rosario: *"[Negro] es el peor color y es feísimo."*	_____	_____
Magdalena: *"Uds. son muy diferentes."*	_____	_____
Magdalena: *"Ella cree que el color negro es el más bonito."*	_____	_____

Sample question:

2. How does the tone expressed in Rosario's letter compare to the tone expressed in Magdalena's letter?
   A Rosario seems more helpful than Magdalena.
   B Magdalena seems more exaggerated than Rosario.
   C Both Rosario and Magdalena have an angry tone in their letters.
   D Magdalena seems more objective than Rosario.

© Pearson Education, Inc. All rights reserved.

Integrated Performance Assessment
Unit theme: En mi dormitorio

Context for the Integrated Performance Assessment: Your Spanish class is going to have a debate. The topic of the debate is the following statement: It is important to clean your bedroom every day.

Interpretive Task: Watch the *Videohistoria: El cuarto de Ignacio* from *Realidades 1, DVD 3, Capítulo 6A* (without the words displayed) and listen to the opinions of Ignacio and his mother. As you listen, think about the debate statement and write down a few ideas that support your opinion.

Interpersonal Task: Explain your opinion to a group of 2 or 3 other students. Listen to the opinions of the other students in your group. Ask questions in order to get more information to help you take a stand in the debate.

Presentational Task: Make an oral presentation to the class in which you take a side on the debate statement and give reasons for your opinion.

Interpersonal Task Rubric

	Score: 1 Does not meet expectations	Score: 3 Meets expectations	Score: 5 Exceeds expectations
Language Use	Student uses little or no target language and relies heavily on native language word order.	Student uses the target language consistently, but may mix native and target language word order.	Student uses the target language exclusively and integrates target language word order into conversation.
Vocabulary Use	Student uses limited and repetitive language.	Student uses only recently acquired vocabulary.	Student uses both recently and previously acquired vocabulary.

Presentational Task Rubric

	Score: 1 Does not meet expectations	Score: 3 Meets expectations	Score: 5 Exceeds expectations
Amount of Communication	Student gives limited arguments to support his/her side.	Student gives adequate arguments to support his/her side.	Student gives consistent arguments to support his/her side.
Accuracy	Student's accuracy with vocabulary and structures is limited.	Student's accuracy with vocabulary and structures is adequate.	Student's accuracy with vocabulary and structures is exemplary.
Comprehensibility	Student's ideas lack clarity and are difficult to understand.	Student's ideas are adequately clear and fairly well understood.	Student's ideas are precise and easily understood.
Vocabulary Use	Student uses limited and repetitive vocabulary.	Student uses only recently acquired vocabulary.	Student uses both recently and previously acquired vocabulary.

© Pearson Education, Inc. All rights reserved.

How "Spanish" Is Spanish Architecture?

1 If you were to travel from the southwestern United States to the southern tip of South America, many buildings would look fairly familiar almost every place you visited. Although regional differences would be obvious, you would still be aware of a certain look shared by many communities in the southwestern United States and Latin America. In large part, that look can be traced to the architecture of Moorish Spain.

2 The Moors were North African Arabs who ruled most of the Iberian Peninsula (Spain and Portugal) for nearly 800 years—from the early eighth century until the late fifteenth century. Many elements of Latin American architecture were first introduced to Spain by the Moors during that period.

3 Patios, for example, became common in cities such as Córdoba and Sevilla beginning in the early eleventh century.

4 Because of widespread political and social unrest during that time, houses were built with heavy doors and thick, fortress-like walls. These walls also helped shield the rooms inside from the sun's heat. The patios, placed in the center of the house and accessible from all first-floor rooms, often had tiled floors. In the center, surrounded by lemon trees and flowers, there was often a pool or a large clay pot filled with cool water. Patios were thus probably the first naturally "air-conditioned" rooms. Throughout Latin America today, as well as in Spain, central patios are still a popular feature of many commercial buildings as well as homes.

5 Another common element of Latin American architecture is the *balcón*, or *mirador*. In Moorish Spain, homes typically had balconies off the second-floor sleeping areas. These balconies, which often included intricately designed wrought iron railings and grates, overlooked the patio. During the period when Latin America was being colonized by Spain, balconies became common in Latin America as well. There was, however, a major difference: most Latin American balconies do not overlook the patio. Instead, they face outward so that people can view the street life of the town.

6 Buildings in Moorish Spain usually differed from those in northern Europe in another way as well. Although wood was used as a building material, it was not nearly as common as stone, brick, and adobe (heavy clay bricks made of sun-dried earth and straw). Today, builders in Latin America and the southwestern United States continue to use many of these same materials and techniques first introduced by the Moors.

© Pearson Education, Inc. All rights reserved.

Answer questions 1–5. Base your answers on the reading *"How 'Spanish' is Spanish Architecture?"*

1 When did the Moors conquer Spain?

     A   in the early 500s

     B   in the early 700s

     C   in the early 800s

     D   in the early 1200s

2 According to the article, what was the main reason why the doors and walls of Spanish homes were so thick during the time of Moorish rule?

     F   They kept the house warm.

     G   They were used for defense and protection.

     H   They enclosed the patio.

     J   The Moors were used to living in homes with thick walls.

3 Which of the following is the best English equivalent of *mirador* in paragraph 4?

     A   a door with a mirror in it

     B   a heavy mirror

     C   a door onto a patio

     D   an overlook

4 Why do architectural features that date to the period of Moorish influence in Spain exist in the southwestern United States and Latin America today?

     F   It gets very hot in those regions.

     G   Those regions were conquered by the Moors.

     H   Those regions were colonized by the Spanish.

     J   There is much political and social unrest in those regions.

5 READ THINK EXPLAIN   Based on what you have read, compare and contrast typical modern homes in Spain and in the United States. What cultural influences might be responsible for these similarities and differences?

© Pearson Education, Inc. All rights reserved.

1 Ⓐ Ⓑ Ⓒ Ⓓ   **2** Ⓕ Ⓖ Ⓗ Ⓙ   **3** Ⓐ Ⓑ Ⓒ Ⓓ

4 Ⓕ Ⓖ Ⓗ Ⓙ

5

READ
THINK
EXPLAIN

_____

_____

_____

_____

_____

_____

_____

_____

_____

_____

© Pearson Education, Inc. All rights reserved.

Synthesizing Information from Multiple Sources to Draw Conclusions

Often readers are asked to look at two or more reading passages and make connections between the different passages. When readers synthesize information, they are forming new ideas based on what they have read in the different reading passages.

Tip

When synthesizing information from various sources, readers benefit when they read actively. While they read, active readers are constantly formulating ideas about how information from various sources relate to each other. Active readers often show these relationships in charts, tables, or graphs.

1. Review **Actividad 28**, *"¿Qué casa están buscando?"* on page 144 in your textbook, and then fill out the chart below.

	What would the house buyer like about Casa Venezia?	What would the house buyer dislike about Casa Venezia?
José Guzmán		
Alejandro Lara		
Dora Peña		

Sample question:

2. Based on the descriptions about the three house buyers and the description of Casa Venezia, which statement below is true?

   A José Guzmán's wife would not like the kitchen at Casa Venezia.

   B Alejandro Lara needs a house like Casa Venezia with its three levels.

   C Dora Peña would have no need for Casa Venezia's carpets in the bedrooms.

   D Casa Venezia seems more suitable for Dora Peña than it does for José Guzmán.

© Pearson Education, Inc. All rights reserved.

Analyzing the Effectiveness of Complex Elements of Plot

When reading stories, it is important for readers to identify the protagonist, or main character, of the story. The protagonist usually has a goal in the story, and it is the protagonist's attempt to reach that goal that moves along the plot of the story. The plot can be summed up as all the actions that occur as the protagonist attempts to reach his or her goal. While attempting to reach his or her goal, the protagonist encounters problems or conflicts that must be resolved. The climax of the story is the point when it becomes clear to the reader that the protagonist will or will not reach his or her goal. Good readers can explain how various elements of the plot such as the protagonist's goals or conflicts affect the outcome of the story.

Tip

1. One way you can identify and understand various plot elements is to use a chart. After reviewing the **Lectura,** *Cantaclara* on pages 146 and 147 in your textbook, fill in the information required in the chart below.

Who is the protagonist?

_____

_____

_____

What is his/her goal?

_____

_____

_____

What conflicts does he/she encounter?

_____

_____

_____

What is the outcome of each conflict?

_____

_____

_____

When is the climax of the story?

_____

_____

_____

Sample question:

2. How would the outcome of the story have been different if Cantaclara had a nice stepmother but a poor singing voice?

   A Cantaclara would have had to let her sisters go with her to *La estrella del futuro.*

   B Cantaclara would have had to clean the kitchen before going to *La estrella del futuro,* but she would not have been a winner.

   C Cantaclara would not have had to clean the kitchen, but she would not have been a winner on *La estrella del futuro.*

   D Cantaclara's mother would have introduced Cantaclara to a handsome prince who would have told Cantaclara that he loved her even without a beautiful singing voice.

© Pearson Education, Inc. All rights reserved.

Integrated Performance Assessment
Unit theme: ¿Cómo es tu casa?

Context for the Integrated Performance Assessment: You usually do chores around the house to help your parents. Now you find yourself in the position of needing money for your personal expenses. You want to convince your parents to give you money and you are willing to do more chores in order to earn money. However, you need some help in planning how to convince your parents.

Interpretive Task: Watch the *Videohistoria: Los quehaceres de Elena* from *Realidades 1, DVD 3, Capítulo 6B* (without the words displayed) to see how Elena negotiates with her little brother, Jorgito. Listen to the chores that Elena does and write down any that you are willing to do.

Interpersonal Task: Discuss your situation with a friend in Spanish class. Explain the extra chores you are willing to do. Ask your friend to suggest additional chores and to help you decide how much money you are going to ask your parents to give you.

Presentational Task: Make an oral presentation to a group of 3 or 4 students in order to rehearse what you plan to say to your parents. Mention at least four chores you are willing to do.

Interpersonal Task Rubric

	Score: 1 Does not meet expectations	Score: 3 Meets expectations	Score: 5 Exceeds expectations
Language Use	Student uses little or no target language and relies heavily on native language word order.	Student uses the target language consistently, but may mix native and target language word order.	Student uses the target language exclusively and integrates target language word order into conversation.
Vocabulary Use	Student uses limited and repetitive language.	Student uses only required acquired vocabulary.	Student uses both recently and previously acquired vocabulary.

Presentational Task Rubric

	Score: 1 Does not meet expectations	Score: 3 Meets expectations	Score: 5 Exceeds expectations
Amount of Communication	Student mentions fewer than four chores that he/she is willing to do.	Student mentions four chores that he/she is willing to do.	Student mentions more than four chores that he/she is willing to do.
Accuracy	Student's accuracy with vocabulary and structures is limited.	Student's accuracy with vocabulary and structures is adequate.	Student's accuracy with vocabulary and structures is exemplary.
Comprehensibility	Student's ideas lack clarity and are difficult to understand.	Student's ideas are adequately clear and fairly well understood.	Student's ideas are precise and easily understood.
Vocabulary Use	Student uses limited and repetitive vocabulary.	Student uses only recently acquired vocabulary.	Student uses both recently and previously acquired vocabulary.

© Pearson Education, Inc. All rights reserved.

Capítulo 6B **Practice Test**

Mi segunda casa es ... ¡una cueva!

1 ¡Hola! Me llamo Macarena y soy española. Vivo con mis padres y tres hermanos en un apartamento grande y bonito en Granada, que está en el sur de España. Pero tenemos otra casa y es... ¡una cueva! Nuestra casa-cueva está cerca de Guadix, un pueblo pintoresco de unos 20.000 habitantes. Guadix está a 60 kilómetros de Granada, y es famoso por sus casas-cueva.

2 Más de un cuarto de la población del pueblo vive en estas casas subterráneas. Tradicionalmente sólo para los pobres y artesanos, hoy día las casas-cueva son la segunda residencia de muchas familias de la clase media. ¡Me encanta pasar tiempo con mi familia en nuestra casa-cueva!

3 ¿Qué tienen de atractivo las casas-cueva?
- La temperatura se mantiene constante (20 grados centígrados) durante todo el año.
- Si la familia necesita más espacio, sólo hay que excavar otro cuarto.

- Tienen todas las comodidades de una casa moderna: dormitorios, cocina, cuarto de baño, sala, comedor, chimenea, electricidad y conexiones para Internet y fax.
- De la puerta hay una magnífica vista. (¡Pocas cuevas tienen ventanas!)

4 Si quieres vivir en un <u>ambiente</u> original, íntimo y rústico, o si simplemente prefieres vivir en otra casa durante el fin de semana o durante las vacaciones de verano, las casas-cueva son perfectas para ti.

© Pearson Education, Inc. All rights reserved.

Realidades **B**

Capítulo 6B   **Practice Test**

Answer questions 1–6. Base your answers on the reading *"Mi segunda casa es... ¡una cueva!"*

1 According to the reading, which of the following statements is false?

    A   Cave houses have all the conveniences of a modern home.

    B   Cave houses are not only for artisans and the poor.

    C   Macarena's family has two homes.

    D   Cave houses offer wonderful views from the windows.

2 From Macarena's description of her family's second home, the reader can conclude that

    F   it gets too hot in Granada during the summer.

    G   her parents are artisans.

    H   she enjoys spending time in the cave.

    J   she doesn't like living in an apartment.

3 In paragraph 4, what does the word *ambiente* mean?

    A   countryside

    B   cave

    C   atmosphere

    D   city

4 Which of the following is <u>not</u> mentioned as an advantage of living in a cave house?

    F   There's a great view from the door.

    G   It's easy to make more furniture from the rocks.

    H   The houses maintain an even temperature all year.

    J   It's easy to add more space to the home.

5 | READ THINK EXPLAIN | Make a list of buildings, vehicles, or places that could be used as homes. Describe the advantages or disadvantages of each one.

6 | READ THINK EXPLAIN | ¿Te gustaría vivir en una casa-cueva? Explica por qué.

© Pearson Education, Inc. All rights reserved.

1 Ⓐ Ⓑ Ⓒ Ⓓ   **2** Ⓕ Ⓖ Ⓗ Ⓙ   **3** Ⓐ Ⓑ Ⓒ Ⓓ

4 Ⓕ Ⓖ Ⓗ Ⓙ

5

READ
THINK
EXPLAIN

_____

_____

_____

_____

_____

6

READ
THINK
EXPLAIN

_____

_____

_____

_____

_____

_____

_____

_____

© Pearson Education, Inc. All rights reserved.

Interpreting Diagrams, Graphs, and Statistical Illustrations

When good readers encounter a diagram, a graph, or any statistical information, they are able to make meaning from what they see. They are able to translate the information that is presented graphically or statistically into useful information. Readers are often asked to make comparisons involving the information in the diagrams, graphs, or statistics.

Tip

One strategy that helps students make meaning from diagrams, graphs, and statistics is to practice translating graphic or statistical information into sentences. In describing relationships that you observe in the diagrams, graphs, or statistics, you should become familiar with making statements with the following words or expressions of comparison:

more than → most   less than → least → fewer than
greater than → larger → largest   smaller → smallest
bigger → biggest   equal → same → different

1. Review **Actividad 10** on page 165 in your textbook. Look at the foreign currency exchange rate data below and then answer the questions that follow.

Foreign Exchange Rates Compared to the U.S. Dollar

Country	Currency	$1 U.S. =	Country	Currency	$1 U.S. =
Argentina	peso	3.0050	Peru	nuevo sol	3.414
Colombia	peso	2274.50	Uruguay	nuevo peso	24.4350
Mexico	peso	10.4730	Venezuela	bolivar	2147.30

Would the shoes in **Actividad 12** that cost 1,820 Uruguayan pesos cost more or less in U.S. dollars? Why?

_____

Are 1,820 Uruguayan pesos worth more or less than 1,820 Mexican pesos? Why?

_____

Which peso (from Argentina, Colombia, Mexico, or Uruguay) could be purchased with the smallest amount of U.S. currency? Why?

Sample question:

2. Based on the information presented in the Foreign Exchange Rate chart above, which statement below is true?

  A When exchanging for U.S. dollars, the Uruguayan nuevo peso is nearly equal in value to the Colombian peso.

  B The number of pesos you would receive in Mexico for 10 U.S. dollars is more than the number of pesos you would receive in Argentina for the same amount of U.S. dollars.

  C One Venezuelan bolivar is equal to 2147.30 U.S. dollars.

  D You would need more Argentinian pesos than Peruvian nuevo soles to buy $1 U.S. dollar.

© Pearson Education, Inc. All rights reserved.

Locates, Gathers, Analyzes, and Evaluates Written Information

By showing that they can locate, gather, analyze, and evaluate information from one or more reading passages, good readers demonstrate that they know how to conduct research. On a test, readers are often asked to locate, gather, analyze, and evaluate information from a reading passage and then show how to put that information to good use.

Tip

Readers who conduct research are skilled at organizing information from their reading. For many, the outline is an excellent way to organize information gathered from research. With an outline, you begin by organizing information into broad categories and then gradually narrow your focus to more specific details.

1. Review the **Lectura**, *Tradiciones de la ropa panameña* on pages 176 and 177 in your textbook and then fill in the missing blanks of the outline below.

Traditional Panamanian Clothing

I _____
   A *Montuna*
   B *De* _____
      1 _____
      2 It costs a lot.
         a _____
         b _____
         c _____
      3 Something that is very important in the city of Las Tablas.

II *La blusa de molas*
   A Made by the Kuna Indians from the San Blas Islands.
   B Molas are decorative panels on the fronts and backs of the blouses.
      1 _____
      2 _____
      3 *Molas* can be found in museums as works of art.

Sample question:

2. If you were interested in making your own samples of traditional Panamanian clothing, all of the following statements would be helpful to you EXCEPT which one?
   A You will need a lot of jewels to decorate a *pollera de gala*.
   B You can show your individual talent and expression with your *molas*.
   C You will discover that the *pollera de gala* is most important in the city of Las Tablas.
   D A *pollera de gala* could require as many as seven months to make by hand.

© Pearson Education, Inc. All rights reserved.

Integrated Performance Assessment
Unit theme: ¿Cuánto cuesta?

Context for the Integrated Performance Assessment: You are planning on going to a special event and want to buy some new clothes to wear.

Interpretive Task: Watch the *Videohistoria: Una noche especial* from *Realidades 1, DVD 4, Capítulo 7A* (without words displayed) as Teresa shops for clothes for a special event. Make a list of the clothes she looks at.

Interpersonal Task: Describe your special event and the new clothes you want to buy to a friend in Spanish class. Ask his/her opinion on the clothes. Then ask him/her for the names of some stores where you should shop for the new clothes.

Presentational Task: Write an e-mail to a friend describing your special event, the new clothes you want to buy, and where you plan to shop. Invite your friend to go with you.

Interpersonal Task Rubric

	Score: 1 Does not meet expectations	Score: 3 Meets expectations	Score: 5 Exceeds expectations
Language Use	Student uses little or no target language and relies heavily on native language word order.	Student uses the target language consistently, but may mix native and target language word order.	Student uses the target language exclusively and integrates target language word order into conversation.
Vocabulary Use	Student uses limited and repetitive language.	Student uses only recently acquired vocabulary.	Student uses both recently and previously acquired vocabulary.

Presentational Task Rubric

	Score: 1 Does not meet expectations	Score: 3 Meets expectations	Score: 5 Exceeds expectations
Amount of Communication	Student gives limited or no details about the special event, the clothes, and the shops.	Student gives adequate details about the special event, the clothes, and the shops.	Student gives consistent details about the special event, the clothes, and the shops.
Accuracy	Student's accuracy with vocabulary and structures is limited.	Student's accuracy with vocabulary and structures is adequate.	Student's accuracy with vocabulary and structures is exemplary.
Comprehensibility	Student's ideas lack clarity and are difficult to understand.	Student's ideas are adequately clear and fairly well understood.	Student's ideas are precise and easily understood.
Vocabulary Use	Student uses limited and repetitive vocabulary.	Student uses only recently acquired vocabulary.	Student uses both recently and previously acquired vocabulary.

© Pearson Education, Inc. All rights reserved.

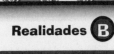
A Culture as Seen Through Its Textiles

1 On July 26, 1925, archaeologists made a dramatic discovery in the desert of the Paracas peninsula, approximately 150 miles south of the Peruvian capital of Lima. In the desert off the Pacific coast they found an underground network of tombs from the Paracas and Nazca cultures that dated back to the fourth century B.C. Such a group of elaborately interconnected tombs is sometimes called a <u>necropolis</u>, a Greek word meaning "city of the dead." The Paracas necropolis contained beautiful, richly decorated gold objects, along with hundreds of perfectly preserved human bodies carefully wrapped in intricately woven, embroidered cloth that was as well preserved as the bodies it contained.

2 Woven cloth, or textiles, has of course played both a practical and a ceremonial role in world cultures for thousands of years. The textiles found at Paracas were probably specially made for use in burials and almost surely revealed the social status of the people buried there.

3 Images woven into garments or added to them were a form of communication in ancient cultures. Whether painted, embroidered, or decorated with metal or brightly colored feathers, many textiles contained important symbolic information. The most common images found on the Paracas textiles were those of birds, cats, snakes, rodents, llamas, and fish. By showing the animals that were native to the region, these pictures represented in one way or another the three basic realms of nature that daily affected the people who made the pictures: the sky, the earth, and the sea. Human forms were also shown. These pictures no doubt reflected concepts important to the culture, such as nature gods, the individual's ancestors, or the individual's social status.

4 Today, people in Peru and neighboring Bolivia continue to weave ponchos, tunics, and hats that use some of the same designs found in their people's textiles over 2,000 years ago.

© Pearson Education, Inc. All rights reserved.

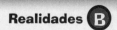

| Capítulo 7A | **Practice Test** |

Answer questions 1–6. Base your answers on the reading *"A Culture as Seen Through Its Textiles."*

1 What is Paracas?

    A   another name for Peru

    B   a Peruvian peninsula and the name of a people who once lived there

    C   the capital of Peru

    D   a type of Peruvian textile

2 What is a <u>necropolis</u>?

    F   a desert in Peru

    G   a place for storing ancient gold objects

    H   a vast underground burial site

    J   a type of Greek city

3 Which one of the following statements is <u>not</u> true?

    A   The modern textiles of Peru are totally different from those found in ancient tombs.

    B   The people of Peru still use many of the same design elements that their ancestors did.

    C   Weaving is a practice that dates back to ancient times.

    D   The tombs in Paracas were discovered in the twentieth century.

4 Why were images included in the textiles of ancient peoples?

    F   for purely religious reasons

    G   to communicate information of some sort

    H   to preserve the body of the person around whom it was wrapped

    J   to impress visitors to the tombs

5 **READ THINK EXPLAIN** "Woven cloth, or textiles, has . . . played both a practical and a ceremonial role in world cultures for thousands of years." Make a list of three "Practical" and three "Ceremonial" uses of textiles today.

6 **READ THINK EXPLAIN** Choose any well-known person and describe the textile that you would design to represent him or her. Describe the symbols (colors, objects, figures) that you would use and explain why you chose them.

© Pearson Education, Inc. All rights reserved.

Communication Workbook

1 Ⓐ Ⓑ Ⓒ Ⓓ **2** Ⓕ Ⓖ Ⓗ Ⓙ **3** Ⓐ Ⓑ Ⓒ Ⓓ

4 Ⓕ Ⓖ Ⓗ Ⓙ

5

READ
THINK
EXPLAIN

_____
_____
_____
_____
_____
_____

6

READ
THINK
EXPLAIN

_____
_____
_____
_____
_____
_____
_____
_____

© Pearson Education, Inc. All rights reserved.

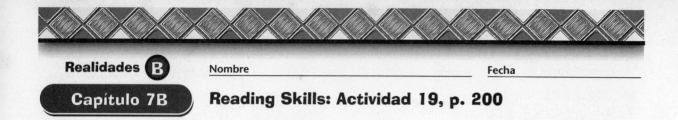

Drawing Conclusions

To draw a conclusion is to form an opinion based on evidence. Sometimes the evidence presented to readers is very limited, but they must ensure that their evidence-based opinions make sense.

Conclusion statements are rarely right or wrong. They are often presented as believable or not. If you are successful at drawing conclusions from your reading, then you likely are skilled at finding evidence in your reading that supports your conclusions.

Conclusions are only as strong as the evidence on which they are based. Conclusions based on little evidence are not as believable as conclusions based on a lot of different kinds of evidence. You must also be willing to change your conclusions as more evidence becomes available in the reading passage.

Tip

One strategy that helps students as they draw conclusions is to use "If-Then" statements with their evidence and conclusions. If a conclusion does not make logical sense, then it will become obvious when presented in an "If-Then" statement. As more evidence is presented in the "If" statements, the conclusions in the "Then" statements will also likely change.

1. On page 200 of your textbook, review **Actividad 19 "Una lección de historia,"** and then complete these statements. Can you draw more than one possible conclusion for the evidence presented below?
   A If in 1848 President James K. Polk paid $15 million dollars to Mexico according to the Treaty of Hidalgo, **and**
   B If in 1898 President William McKinley helped Cuba and Puerto Rico declare their independence from Spain, **then** one could conclude that

   _____

                                      or

   _____.

   Now add this third piece of evidence:
   C If in 1904 President Theodore Roosevelt began building the Panama Canal, **then** based on points **A, B,** and **C,** one could conclude that American presidents

   _____

   _____.

Sample question:

2. If Columbus discovered the Dominican Republic in 1492 and if Juan Ponce de León explored Florida in 1513, then one could conclude that
   A both Columbus and de León were motivated by the desire to find gold.
   B the Dominican Republic and Florida had a lot in common during the 1500's.
   C Spain was active in exploration of the Americas in the late fifteenth and early sixteenth centuries.
   D neither Columbus nor de León discovered the fountain of youth in the New World.

© Pearson Education, Inc. All rights reserved.

Determining Main Idea

To determine the main idea of a reading passage, the reader must be able to describe what a reading passage is mostly about. He or she should be able to summarize the main idea of the reading passage in one sentence. A common problem for students when working with this skill is confusing an important detail in the reading passage with the main idea. Just because something is mentioned in the reading passage does not mean it is the main idea of the passage. Many times the main idea is not even stated in the reading passage. This is often called an implied main idea. No matter if the main idea is stated or implied, the basic question remains the same: "What is this reading passage mostly about?"

Tip

One common mistake that students make with main-idea questions is that they often choose main-idea statements that are either too broad or too narrow. When you are too broad in your thinking, you are too general and do not recognize what is unique about the particular reading passage. When you are too narrow, you focus too much on isolated details without looking at the whole picture.

1. Review the **Lectura, *¡De compras!*** on pages 208 and 209 of your textbook. Then read the main-idea statements listed below and indicate if they are too broad, too narrow, or just right.

   _____ Little Havana is the heart of the Cuban community in Miami.

   _____ Shopping is a fun activity.

   _____ United States cities with large Hispanic communities offer interesting shopping opportunities.

   _____ Hispanic residents of the United States love to go shopping.

   _____ Olvera Street is the oldest street in Los Angeles and the place to see Mexican culture.

   _____ One can find inexpensive and unique things to buy in the Hispanic neighborhoods of American cities.

Sample question:

2. Another good title for the reading passage "*¡De compras!*" would be
   A "Guava Paste on Miami's Eighth Street."
   B "Shopping Adventures in America's Hispanic Neighborhoods."
   C "Trying to Find Original Products at Good Prices."
   D "What to Buy in Los Angeles and San Antonio."

© Pearson Education, Inc. All rights reserved.

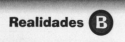

Integrated Performance Assessment
Unit theme: ¡Qué regalo!

Context for the Integrated Performance Assessment: A group of students from Colombia is coming to spend three weeks in your school. They want to know where to shop and what to buy in your community so that they can buy gifts for friends and family.

Interpretive Task: Read the *Lectura: ¡De compras!* on pages 208–209 of *Realidades B* to see how the shops and shopping areas of four cities are described. As you read, think about the shops and shopping areas in your community. Write down the names of four shops in your community and a brief description of what each shop sells.

Interpersonal Task: Discuss your ideas about the shops and what they sell with your partner. Working together, select three shops that you think the students from Colombia would like.

Presentational Task: Send an e-mail to one of the students from Colombia describing the three shops that you and your partner selected. Tell him/her what each shop sells and why you think he/she will like each shop.

Interpersonal Task Rubric

	Score: 1 Does not meet expectations	Score: 3 Meets expectations	Score: 5 Exceeds expectations
Language Use	Student uses little or no target language and relies heavily on native language word order.	Student uses the target language consistently, but may mix native and target language word order.	Student uses the target language exclusively and integrates target language word order into conversation.
Vocabulary Use	Student uses limited and repetitive language.	Student uses only recently acquired vocabulary.	Student uses both recently and previously acquired vocabulary.

Presentational Task Rubric

	Score: 1 Does not meet expectations	Score: 3 Meets expectations	Score: 5 Exceeds expectations
Amount of Communication	Student gives limited or no details about the three shops, what they sell, and why the visiting student would like the shops.	Student gives adequate details about the three shops, what they sell, and why the visiting student would like the shops.	Student gives consistent details about the three shops, what they sell, and why the visiting student would like the shops.
Accuracy	Student's accuracy with vocabulary and structures is limited.	Student's accuracy with vocabulary and structures is adequate.	Student's accuracy with vocabulary and structures is exemplary.
Comprehensibility	Student's ideas lack clarity and are difficult to understand.	Student's ideas are adequately clear and fairly well understood.	Student's ideas are precise and easily understood.
Vocabulary Use	Student uses limited and repetitive vocabulary.	Student uses only recently acquired vocabulary.	Student uses both recently and previously acquired vocabulary.

© Pearson Education, Inc. All rights reserved.

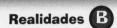
Practice Test

Necesito comprar ropa

¿Te gusta ir de compras, pero no te gusta estar con muchas personas?
Lee este artículo de la solución de Margarita para este problema.

1   Margarita, una joven argentina de dieciséis años, tiene un problema. Necesita comprar ropa para sus vacaciones en Chile, pero está muy ocupada. No le gusta ir al centro comercial porque siempre hay muchas personas por allí. Decide visitar uno de los sitios en el Internet para buscar la ropa que necesita.

2   Primero, Margarita busca un sitio donde se especializan en ropa para jóvenes. El sitio que más le gusta tiene un catálogo con mucha variedad de ropa moderna. En la página principal, hay información sobre cómo seleccionar el departamento donde quiere comprar unos artículos. Esa página indica cómo pagar por lo que compra y cómo comunicarse con la compañía. También incluye información sobre garantías, descuentos y qué opciones tiene si no le gusta lo que compra.

3   Margarita selecciona dos jeans, tres camisetas de diferentes colores, dos pantalones cortos, un suéter negro, una sudadera morada, una chaqueta y unos zapatos. También compra el especial de la semana, una minifalda azul que cuesta sólo veinte pesos. ¡Perfecto!

4   Luego, Margarita tiene una pregunta: "¿Cómo puedo determinar si esta ropa y estos zapatos me van a quedar bien?" Decide consultar la página donde hay información para ayudar a los clientes a determinar esto.

5   Después, Margarita decide pagar por toda la ropa con su tarjeta de crédito, pero tiene otra pregunta: "¿Garantiza este sitio la protección de mi información personal?" Consulta otra página donde informan a los clientes que sí hay protección.

6   Cuando la ropa llega a su casa, Margarita está muy contenta. Toda la ropa que compró le queda bien y los colores son brillantes.

© Pearson Education, Inc. All rights reserved.

Capítulo 7B   **Practice Test**

Answer questions 1–6. Base your answers on the reading *"Necesito comprar ropa."*

1 What is Margarita's problem?

    A   She needs clothes for her vacation but doesn't have enough money to buy them.

    B   She needs clothes for her vacation but doesn't like to shop in crowded malls.

    C   She needs to replace the clothes that she lost during her vacation.

    D   She needs to buy vacation clothes before the stores close.

2 What type of information is <u>not</u> mentioned on the main page of the Web site that Margarita consults?

    F   how to pay for your purchases

    G   how to choose the department you're interested in

    H   which items are discounted

    J   which items are no longer available

3 According to the article, why is Margarita concerned about ordering from an online catalog?

    A   She's worried that she won't receive the items on time.

    B   She's worried that her personal information might not be protected.

    C   She's worried that she can't return the items if she's unhappy with them.

    D   She's worried that the items might look different from the way they look in the catalog.

4 How does Margarita feel after the package arrives?

    F   unhappy because it didn't arrive on time

    G   unhappy because the clothes did not fit well

    H   happy because the clothes fit well and the colors were bright

    J   happy because the company included a special gift in the package

5 READ THINK EXPLAIN   ¿Prefieres ir de compras en un centro comercial o en el Internet? ¿Por qué?

6 READ THINK CREATE   Imagina que vas a crear un sitio en el Internet para ropa deportiva para jóvenes. Inventa un nombre para el sitio, decide qué tipo de información vas a incluir en la página principal, qué tipos de fotos o dibujos vas a incluir y cuánto cuesta cada artículo de ropa. En tu hoja de papel, dibuja la página principal de tu sitio. Debes dibujar una página atractiva que a los estudiantes de tu escuela les gustaría visitar.

        Communication Workbook

© Pearson Education, Inc. All rights reserved.

1 Ⓐ Ⓑ Ⓒ Ⓓ   **2** Ⓕ Ⓖ Ⓗ Ⓙ   **3** Ⓐ Ⓑ Ⓒ Ⓓ

4 Ⓕ Ⓖ Ⓗ Ⓙ

5

READ
THINK
EXPLAIN

_____
_____
_____
_____
_____
_____

6

READ
THINK
CREATE

© Pearson Education, Inc. All rights reserved.

Analyzing the Validity and Reliability of Information

When good readers analyze information for validity and reliability, one of the most important questions that they ask themselves about what they have read is "How do I know that I can trust that this information is true or accurate?" After answering this question, readers need to determine how such information can be used.

Tip

One way readers check information in a reading passage for validity and reliability is to ask, "How could I verify that this information is accurate or true?" Some ways to verify this include observing, taking measurements, conducting experiments, getting advice from experts in that particular field, and interviewing people with firsthand experience.

1. On page 227 of your textbook, review **Actividad 12 *"¿Quieres aprender a bucear?"*** Then read the statements below from this activity and explain how, if at all, you could verify their truth or accuracy.

   ¡Aprende a bucear en sólo tres cursos!

   _____

   _____

   Practica un deporte interesante y divertido.

   _____

   _____

   Pasa tiempo en un lugar fantástico.

   _____

   _____

   Hay un lenguaje especial que permite a los buzos comunicarse en el agua con señales.

   _____

   _____

   En los cursos de buceo, puedes aprender estas señales.

   _____

   _____

Sample question:

2. If you were using the brochure for *Escuela de buceo "Flor del mar"* for a research project about scuba diving in the Dominican Republic, which information seems least reliable?

   A Scuba diving is an interesting and fun sport.

   B You can learn hand signals in the diving courses, and this will help you as a diver.

   C You can learn to scuba dive after only three classes.

   D One of the most important hand signals for scuba divers is "Danger!"

© Pearson Education, Inc. All rights reserved.